The Rise and Fall of the Student Nonviolent Coordinating Committee

by
Martin Oppenheimer

This book would not have been produced without the
encouragement and production assistance of Jai Breeze
Abbott and Miriam L.E. Oppenheimer. Footnotes
follow page 91.
Publication (2024)
-*THREE ARROWS PRESS*-

Preface

We were among the dozens of German-Jewish refugee families from Nazi Germany who ended up becoming chicken farmers in semi-rural South Jersey during the War. A school bus took me to a Middle School for my eighth grade. One day around Easter time, I heard a shout directed at me: "Christ killer." Yes, the old libel from the Middle Ages came from my neighbors' children while the war against the Nazi state was still underway.

There had been no Black people in the local town, but one day the school bus stopped at a driveway leading to a large farm to pick up two Black kids, maybe eight or nine years old. The white kids on the bus loudly erupted with the N-word while the two Black kids hovered, frightened, in their seats. I got up and loudly over the noise said "Why are you yelling at them? They've done nothing to you!" Some of the white kids then turned on me, calling me a "N-lover." I had never heard that expression. I learned later in my college sociology class what I had done: I had "identified with the oppressed."

Sociology opened the door to learning more about both oppressors like the local kids on the bus and what they represented on a larger scale, and the oppressed, like the new kids and the millions who looked like them. I joined my University's National Association for the Advancement of Colored People club. In 1953 I was drafted into the tail-end of the Korean War and spent nine months stationed in Alabama. If you had eyes, you could see in the neighboring towns the realities of full-scale racial segregation, though as a Northern white soldier you should, for your safety, ignore it.

A few years later, just as I was searching for a Ph.D. dissertation topic within the broad field of what was not yet called African-American studies, it dropped into my lap: The Sit-In Movement of "Negro" (not yet Black) students in the South had just begun.

*

The Civil Rights Movement of the 1960s brought the Cold War freeze in American politics to an end. The Montgomery Bus Boycott, led by Martin Luther King Jr., initiated on Dec. 1, 1955, shattered all the "end of ideology" propaganda being promoted by status quo social scientists. A series of direct-action demonstrations to integrate public facilities, some preceding Montgomery, started to pick up steam in the late 1950s, and hope for wider reforms changed from a mere flicker to the realization that we were on the brink of seeing something miraculous: a mass interracial movement to destroy racial segregation in the United States.

The Sit-ins that became a Movement began on Feb. 1, 1960, in Greensboro, N.C. They quickly spread from Greensboro to dozens of cities in the Upper South. Their recruits mainly came from traditional Black colleges and universities. In Philadelphia, I participated in organizing a student group to help civil rights organizations picket local branches of department stores that were the targets of sit-ins in the South. In April, I attended the founding meeting of what would become the Student Nonviolent Coordinating Committee, in Raleigh, North Carolina. In October, I went to Atlanta, Georgia, as a delegate to SNCC's second conference, in the company of several young socialists. In the Winter and Spring of 1961, I traveled to ten Southern cities as a "participant-observer" to gather more information for the research that would become my doctoral dissertation, later published as *The Sit-In Movement of 1960* (Carlson, 1989). Whenever civil rights activists were demonstrating in a community on my itinerary, I joined in.

I joined the Philadelphia chapter of the Congress of Racial Equality, which was heavily involved in supporting the southern students. Soon CORE in the North began to tackle local issues: police brutality, poor housing, poor schools, unemployment. We conducted sit-ins to promote equal employment opportunities on city construction projects. In 1964 I was a delegate to the CORE convention and remember hearing the chilling news of the three missing Freedom Summer volunteers. Given what we knew of the repressive atmosphere of the South, it was taken for granted that they had been murdered. In the summer of 1965, at its Durham, North Carolina convention, where I was also a delegate, CORE moved in a distinctly Black Power direction and whites began to be excluded. Soon most whites who had been active in civil rights shifted their attention to the American war in Vietnam.

Many who participated in the civil rights movement of the 1960s are still politically active in the vast number of causes that are the logical consequence of capitalism's decay and continuing racist practices. Alas, our numbers decline week by week. We will not live long enough to see the end, whether it be the destruction of humankind by fire or water or nuclear disaster, or its transformation into a humane, democratic, cooperative society. The demonstrations that periodically shake the pillars of the temples of capital around the world may be the beginnings of larger movements for fundamental social change. Hopefully, the organizations and parties that will grow from these recent new beginnings will be better able to defend themselves against the inevitable strategies of the agents of the status quo: cooptation and repression, than their predecessors. Hopefully, they will avoid the kinds of internal conflicts that contributed to the destruction of SNCC, Students for a Democratic Society (SDS), CORE, and others. Perhaps this volume will help the politically engaged reader to understand more about what succeeded and what to avoid.

This book is one sociologist's attempt at a "critical" interpretation of the events of only a few short years in the long history of the Freedom Movement. It is an attempt to describe not only the heroic side of SNCC but also some of the cruel realities that hemmed it in and helped to undermine and ultimately destroy it.

I have benefited greatly from the experience of writing the story of SNCC. I have been humbled by the courage of so many who were direct participants in the struggle. I thank them and express my appreciation to those whose writings have helped me. The idea for this book came from a German friend who was a volunteer in Freedom Summer. We were to write it together for a German publisher, but that was not to be. I dedicate this volume to his memory: Helmut Reinicke (1941-2018), social-historian, philosopher, adventurer, revolutionary.

Table Of Contents

Chapter 1
History: How We Got To Greensboro

"It was believed by most well-meaning people that self-healing would work, that the Negro problem would come to solve itself by the lapse of time." Gunnar Myrdal, An American Dilemma, *v. II, Harper & Brothers, 1944.*

The Student Nonviolent Coordinating Committee (SNCC) was an outgrowth of the sit-in movement that began on Feb. 1, 1960. Its founding convention took place at Shaw University in Raleigh, North Carolina April 15-17 of that year. More than 200 delegates representing student civil rights organizations at 52 colleges and high schools attended. By the summer of 1964, SNCC was able to mobilize approximately 1250 staff and volunteers for the famous "Freedom Summer." That Fall SNCC counted 160 full-time staff.

Thirteen years later, in December 1973, the New York office of the Federal Bureau of Investigation ended its surveillance of SNCC and closed its file, noting there had been no activity for several years "and that future prospects for such are exceedingly faint."[1]

What happened? What was SNCC? How did SNCC come about? What led to its triumphs, and what led to its demise? This volume will try to answer those questions.

We think of the 1960 sit-ins as the trigger event that led to many subsequent developments in the broader civil rights movement, indeed as a turning point in black, and more generally, U.S. history. But the sit-ins, SNCC, and the civil rights movement of the 1960s more generally, had their origins in vast social changes that began long before.[2]

*

In the years immediately following World War II, the war against fascism, the U.S. South had more in common with South Africa than it had with the U.S. North. More than half of all Blacks were living in rural areas. A "Black Belt" of counties in which Blacks were the majority or close to it, ran from rural Maryland to East Texas. Their political influence in this belt was nil. Even a decade later, in the Presidential election of 1956, Louisiana had four counties in which Blacks were 61 to 73% of the population, and not one was registered to vote. In 1947 there were only 595,000 Blacks registered in the eleven Southern states, out of about 5 million of voting age. The U.S. Commission on Civil Rights reported in 1961 that not only were Blacks effectively disfranchised in some 100 counties over eight Southern states, but that the "Negro population suffers extensive deprivation—legal, economic, educational, and social."[3] In 1950 about 20% of Blacks in the Southern states were still working in agriculture, twice the white rate; the majority of these were day laborers. Conditions little short of serfdom and peonage were typical for many Black people in rural areas. This agricultural Black proletariat was integral to the economic structure of the South, which could reasonably be viewed as a neo-colony or branch-plant of the North, a classic example of third world "dependent development." Segregation functioned to maintain a low-paid Black labor force in both agriculture and industry and to keep Black and white workers from uniting around common issues.

Yet the seeds of change had already been planted; the structures of dependent development had begun to crack 17 years earlier, during the Depression, with the creation of the Tennessee Valley Authority. The TVA, an autonomous publicly-owned institution created by the New Deal, electrified, literally, many parts of the South, promoting the beginnings of an infrastructure for industrial development. This in turn enabled Southern industry to play its part in war production during World War II. The gradual shift of proletarianization from rural to urban-industrial was underway.

In the South Atlantic states, 18.7% of the Black population lived in urban areas in 1900. By 1950 it was 48%. The "Black Belt" of Deep South plantation counties was rapidly shrinking, due in part to the mechanization of cotton picking, which displaced Black labor and pushed Blacks both Northward and to Southern urban areas. The Black petty bourgeoisie of merchants, clergy, and other professionals grew. Black-owned newspapers and radio stations proliferated. This differentiated, urbanized class structure was able to create economic reserves, enabling more Blacks to enter (segregated) universities, which became breeding grounds for intellectual ferment and protest. Urban Black workers' contacts with labor unions, some of them led by radicals, increased. The ambitions of the Black bourgeoisie, combined with the material interests of the Black

3

community, promoted increased participation in the political process in the urban South. Black voting in the North was already extensive, and Black political organizations (mainly components of Democratic Party urban "machines") were not without influence on white Democratic politicians. There were by then several Black members of the House of Representatives from the North.

Even in the South, Black voter registration had doubled from 1947 to 1958. Indeed, in the Deep Southern state of Alabama, it went from a mere 6,000 to 70,000, and in Mississippi from 5,000 to 20,000—a pittance, of course, compared to the number of adult Black citizens who were still prevented from registering to vote by one stratagem or another, including violence by the authorities or by mobs. Black voter registration was heavily concentrated in urban areas.

Yet Mississippi, on the eve of 1964's "Freedom Summer," was an exception to this relative progress. Here cotton farming was far less mechanized and dependent on cheap labor. Nearly 70% of Blacks still lived in rural areas, and more than one-third of Black workers still worked in agriculture, twice the rate for the rest of the South. Living conditions for Blacks were far worse, poverty was much more extreme than elsewhere in the South. In 1962 there were five counties with Black majorities and no Blacks registered to vote.[4]

The civil rights movement that we associate with the 1960s was the culmination of this vast set of social and economic changes, in which Mississippi was an anomaly. Yet by 1960 conditions for Blacks in the other Southern

4

states were better only in degree. The tradition of Black struggle itself, going back to the very beginnings of slavery in the New World was also part of the context for the new movement. Even the failed movement to stop "Jim Crow" legislation, which imposed segregation in the South following Reconstruction, resulted in the founding of the National Association for the Advancement of Colored People by Blacks and radical whites in the 1905-1908 period. The Garvey "back to Africa" movement of the 1920s provided tens of thousands of Blacks with organizing experience. In December 1955 the Montgomery Bus Boycott, led by Rev. Martin Luther King, Jr. began. In 1957 Congress, under the Republican Eisenhower administration, passed the first civil rights bill since 1875 (it empowered the federal government to enforce voting rights but, alas, required offenders to be prosecuted before local juries, which in the South generally excluded Blacks and thus inevitably acquitted the accused). In that year and again in 1958 and 1959 there were demonstrations in Washington demanding implementation of court decisions on school integration. There were sporadic sit-ins to integrate public facilities including restaurants and amusement parks. One of the earliest was in Chicago in 1942, organized by the Congress of Racial Equality (CORE), but the first recorded sit-ins by Black students were in Oklahoma City, Oklahoma, and in Wichita, Kansas, both in August 1958.

By 1960 there were 1.5 million registered black voters in the eleven states of the South, enough to constitute critical margins for President Kennedy's victory in several of them.

At 4:30 p.m. on Feb. 1, 1960, four male students from the predominantly Black North Carolina Agricultural and Technical College entered the F.W. Woolworth store in downtown Greensboro, North Carolina, and sat down to wait for service.[5] There was no service, and there were no incidents. After the first day, they came back with other students. After the first two days, women from the traditionally Black Bennett College joined. The four men approached the head of the local branch of the National Association for the Advancement of Colored People (NAACP), who in turn contacted the national office of the Congress of Racial Equality (CORE). A white organizer was sent to Greensboro and he talked with the students, briefing them on the principles and tactics of nonviolent action techniques. By this time, the sit-in had been picked up by the press and radio. The movement was underway.

The Greensboro sit-ins occurred in an environment that in hindsight was perfect for the "take-off" of the movement. Greensboro is located in a part of the state historically opposed to the segregationist Democratic Party dominated "Black Belt" plantation counties. Only 25% of the Greensboro population was Black, hence not a major threat to the political order. Aside from North Carolina Agricultural and Technical College, there were four other colleges in Greensboro. There was an NAACP Branch; there was contact with CORE. These resources were essential.

The Greensboro sit-ins "triggered" similar demonstrations throughout the South and border states such as Maryland. Within the first week the sit-in idea, carried by press and radio reports primarily, reached Durham and Winston-Salem, North Carolina. Eleven of the first fifteen sit-ins were within 100 miles of Greensboro. One observer pointed out that North Carolina A&T's basketball team played five games in two weeks and apparently spread the word. Students at each of the five opposing schools engaged in sit-ins. Within two weeks the demonstrations leaped state lines into Virginia and South Carolina and on February 13th, to Nashville, Tennessee, and Tallahassee, Florida. In a period of sixty days, the sit-ins had spread to nearly eighty communities as far removed as Xenia, Ohio, and Sarasota, Florida. Nearly half of all communities that would have sit-ins had them in this period. By August, some segregated facilities had been integrated into 27 communities of the Upper South. In March 1961, CORE was able to announce that 138 communities had integrated at least some facilities, often despite intense hostility and brutal attacks on the nonviolent demonstrators by some segments of the population, especially white youths.

Local politicians and merchants were under considerable pressure in many cities of the Upper South as the demonstrations spread. First, the nonviolent demonstrators disrupted normal business and threatened financial losses. And second, the disturbances caused by segregationists created a climate considered not conducive to investment by outside (Northern) corporations. This pressure created an incentive for the settlement of the disputes, that is, the integration of at

7

least some public facilities. It was clear to many white community leaders that such integration would not in any way challenge the basic power structures or property relations of these communities.

Nearly 1,000 Blacks and white sympathizers were arrested during the first two months of sit-ins. Hundreds of students suffered tear gas, police dogs, burning cigars on clothing, and beatings. Dozens were suspended or expelled from schools.

In the Deep Southern states of South Carolina, Georgia, Mississippi, Alabama, and Louisiana, the nonviolent movement and its community allies met with intense repression. Under such virtually police state conditions, organizing nonviolent direct action (sit-ins in the main in 1960) required immense courage by Black students and their community supporters, and in fact, there were communities with Black colleges where fear predominated. All the more remarkable that demonstrations did take place in places like Montgomery, Alabama (where the police department was heavily Ku Klux Klan), Columbia, South Carolina (where on one occasion 192 students were arrested while marching around the State Capitol), and Orangeburg, South Carolina (where some 500 students were arrested and hosed down in freezing weather).

Resistance to the movement was most intense when Blacks were close to outnumbering, or actually did outnumber whites. Here larger proportions of the labor force, both white and Black, were still in agriculture, although there were enclaves of Blacks who owned their own farms and would prove reliable allies to SNCC organizers involved in voter registration very soon. Integration of any facilities, not to mention voting, was viewed by most whites as a threat to the basic social and political order, not without reason. Black participation in elections would (and ultimately did) lead to the election of Black mayors, sheriffs, and other local, state, and soon enough federal offices. But in the early 1960s that was still in the future and resistance by local and state authorities, backed by mob violence and the Ku Klux Klan, was the common response to any effort to integrate any institution.

Chapter 2

On to Mississippi

"Weapons: Tear Gas: Chloroacetophenone (CS) or Diphenylamine (DM, or Adamsite) are termed "harassing agents" and are usually used in grenade form to demoralize, panic, and disperse crowds, mobs, and demonstrations There is no defense against gas attack except masks or leaving the area Retreat in an orderly fashion from the scene" Excerpt from A Manual for Direct Action*, used in training for Freedom Summer, Chapter 8: Counter-Demonstration Operations.*

As the sit-ins spread throughout the South, it became obvious to some of the veterans of earlier civil rights struggles that training and coordination were needed sooner rather than later. The Highlander Folk School in Tennessee, an old-time leadership training school active in adult education especially for the labor movement sponsored an integrated college workshop on the first weekend of April 1960. About a hundred students from nineteen states participated in workshops and learned labor and civil rights songs from the past that would become part of SNCC's and others' itineraries. A year earlier Highlander had been forced to close and reopen in another location after a police raid and some convictions on a variety of fabricated minor charges. It acquired a radical reputation since it admitted anyone who chose to come to its training sessions, including Communists. But then, any institution advocating an end to segregation was considered radical if not Communist by the general white population and the establishment media of the time in the South.

In further response to the need for coordination, the Southern Christian Leadership Conference (SCLC), a federation of local "adult" civil rights groups, secured the cooperation of CORE, the American Friends Service Committee (AFSC) (Quakers), and the Fellowship of Reconciliation (FoR), a pacifist group, to sponsor a "Leadership Conference in Nonviolent Resistance." The Conference began on April 15 at Shaw University in Raleigh, North Carolina, the state capital. A number of civil rights figures who were already well-known addressed the 200-plus participants, including Martin Luther King Jr., James Lawson from Nashville, Tennessee, the "dean" of the conference, and Ella Baker, SCLC's Executive Secretary. In Lawson's keynote speech he called *Crisis*, the official publication of the National Association for the Advancement of Colored People (NAACP) the magazine of the "black bourgeois club." Baker, in attempting to paper over the controversy, told the press the only difference between SCLC and the NAACP was one of emphasis.[1] On its last day, April 17, 1960, the conference established a coordinating committee, initially called a "temporary" committee, and adopted a statement of purpose (see Appendix). This was the official start of SNCC.

In May, a sub-group of around a dozen students who had attended the Raleigh conference had a meeting that included Rev. Martin Luther King Jr., Ella Baker, and others in Atlanta, Georgia. The students set up an office. Marion Barry, from Fisk University, was selected chairman. The choice of Barry symbolized two things: Barry was a Southerner; the movement was to be

11

Southern. And, he was not a minister, a deliberate move by the students in reaction to the "quasi-religious orientation of the movement" influenced by the SCLC and King.[2] (Barry would become Mayor of Washington, D.C. years later.) In June the organization, still called the Temporary Student Nonviolent Coordinating Committee, hired its first full-time, paid staff member. She was Jane Stembridge, a white Southerner and graduate of Union Theological Seminary in New York City.

By the end of May 1960, many Upper South business people had come to realize that the cost of not desegregating facilities was greater than the cost of desegregation, and many communities created bi-racial commissions to negotiate settlements. By October, 29 cities had such commissions, often intended to co-opt and thwart desegregation efforts. However, students and their community allies, bolstered by boycotts of the segregated chain stores, including their Northern branches, continued the pressure throughout the summer. By August, 27 Southern cities and counties, plus a number of "Northern" communities such as Las Vegas, Nevada, had desegregated at least some facilities.

But now SNCC and its allies were faced with the much more difficult problem of how to handle the harder centers of resistance in the Deep South states, where virtually no desegregation had taken place. At the same time, they had to decide what to do with the local affiliates that had won their victories. The answer, as it slowly developed, can be summed up in the term Political Action, in which SNCC's role was to lead the drive to register Black voters in the Deep South. First, however, in August student groups conducted demonstrations at both Democratic and Republican Presidential Conventions. SNCC sent spokespeople to both parties' conventions asking for "platform planks" supporting a range of civil rights reforms from implementation of school desegregation court decisions to equal job opportunities to the unhampered exercise of the right to register and vote. Both parties actually passed resolutions that at least in general terms supported such rights. Such pressure on conventions and rhetorical support for many kinds of reforms were by no means unusual; such "planks" were a normal part of all parties' "platforms," and in general were understood (even by the public) to be little more than window-dressing.

By the time school resumed in the Fall of 1960, SNCC had become the public image of the Southern student movement, and it was the apparatus that directed, or at least coordinated, local student protest groups.

On October 19, 31 demonstrators including Rev. Martin Luther King Jr. were arrested in Atlanta, Georgia at a department store sit-in. King and the others were sent to prison. Democratic Party presidential candidate John F. Kennedy telephoned his personal sympathy to King's wife, and the local judge was persuaded to release everyone. The Republican candidate, Richard Nixon, was silent on the issue. Kennedy won the election by a very narrow margin, generally attributed to a significant swing by Black voters from their traditional Republican affiliation (due to the fact that the Southern Democrats were then and always had been segregationist, and the Republican Party was the Party of Abraham Lincoln) to the Democratic side.

SNCC had held a convention just a few days before the arrests in Atlanta. Here the basic issue of structure was raised for the first time: how much autonomy for local groups should there be relative to centralized coordination? A compromise was devised by which "protest areas" composed of local groups within one or several nearby communities would be the basic unit of voting. At this point, SNCC still maintained a staff of one administrative secretary plus its office in Atlanta, supported financially by "adult" groups and private donations. There were 25 members of the "Committee," 17 of whom were delegates from various Southern and border states and Washington, D.C. Three national student groups also had votes. The Committee met about every two months to coordinate, in a loose way, its constituent parts. Local groups remained largely autonomous. Over the next several years this structure would be debated and would change, with profound implications for SNCC's survival. By now, SNCC was no longer "temporary."

The sit-ins continued in those communities that had strong student organizations. SNCC officially called for a "second phase" of coordinated stand-ins at movie theaters for Feb. 1, 1961, the first anniversary of the sit-ins in Greensboro. A sit-in also took place at the offices of Paramount, the film company, in New York City.

With the turn of the year the condition of Blacks in Fayette and Haywood Counties, Tennessee, came to the attention of civil rights groups. Mostly tenant farmers, share-croppers, and small-holding farmers,[3] a number of the Blacks in counties near the Mississippi River had been expelled from their lands as part of a campaign led

14

by the local White Citizens Councils[4] to discourage them from voting. As a result, hundreds of families faced the winter without food or shelter. Assistance poured in from sympathetic groups and a "tent city" was constructed. By the Summer of 1961, following a lawsuit by the U.S. Justice Department, most of the farmers had returned to the land. SNCC was not directly involved in this campaign. But several figures who would play important roles in SNCC were, notably James Forman, who had been sent to help by Chicago CORE. When Forman's job was done in Fayette and Haywood Counties, he immediately headed for Nashville, where SNCC was now coordinating the continuation of the Freedom Rides. Later in the year Forman, who was an Air Force veteran, and older than most of the students, would become SNCC's next Executive Secretary.

CORE, with a long history of nonviolent campaigns against segregation, decided, in the winter of 1961, to test Court rulings banning segregation in interstate travel. On May 4 thirteen volunteers (seven Blacks and six whites) set forth from Washington, D.C. headed for New Orleans in two buses intending to integrate segregated eating and bathroom facilities at southern bus terminals. Two of the seven Blacks belonged to SNCC affiliates. One was John Lewis, who would become SNCC chairman and much later a member of the U.S. House of Representatives.

The "Freedom Riders" were assaulted first in Rock Hill, South Carolina. Then on May 14, a white mob attacked the buses in Anniston, Alabama. One bus was burned, the mob beating the riders as they fled. When the other bus arrived in Anniston, the mob broke into the bus and viciously assaulted the riders. That bus managed to continue to Birmingham, where a white mob attacked the riders as they debarked for the waiting room of the terminal. The police were absent. CORE was forced to discontinue the ride because no bus driver could be found to take the riders further. But now students in Nashville, Tennessee, vowed to continue the ride, and on May 17 a group took a bus to Birmingham, Alabama. All ten students (including two whites) were promptly arrested and a day later escorted to the Tennessee border. An attempt to return to Birmingham was thwarted again because no bus driver was willing to take the risk.

By this time Robert F. Kennedy, the Attorney General, had intervened with the Alabama governor, and on May 20 a group of riders left Birmingham for Montgomery, the state capital, escorted by police. The police disappeared as the bus approached Montgomery, and when the bus arrived, a white mob attacked the riders and a white Justice Department official. Kennedy then sent federal marshals in case of further trouble. However, the following evening, when the riders and local Blacks assembled to hear Rev. Martin Luther King Jr. speak in a local church, whites began to riot outside, forcing the congregants to remain inside for the night. The governor of the state at first refused to intervene, but at the threat of federal troops being sent finally declared martial law and state troopers dispersed the mob. Several days later the Freedom Ride did continue to Jackson, Mississippi, accompanied by six white national guardsmen. Police arrested the riders when they attempted to desegregate the "white" restroom at the terminal, and riders in a second bus were also arrested. More and more freedom riders arrived in Jackson over the summer and more than 300 were arrested, most choosing "jail, not bail." Many ended up at the notorious Parchman Farm prison on sixty-day sentences. Finally, later that Fall, the Interstate Commerce Commission issued a new ruling banning segregated facilities in bus and train terminals, although enforcement was feeble.

Voter registration soon became SNCC's priority. In August and September 1961, SNCC workers went to rural Mississippi to persuade local Blacks to register. Progress in the face of assaults by local whites, including officials, and arrests, was impossible. On August 15, SNCC worker Bob Moses was jailed for two days; following his release he was assaulted and severely beaten. His assailant was arrested but acquitted by an all-white jury. In McComb, Mississippi, arrests and assaults followed a Black student rally at the City Hall. Bob Zellner, a white SNCC worker who was a native Alabaman, was beaten and severely injured. He, two other SNCC workers, and nine local Blacks were sentenced to four months in jail for disturbing the peace. On Sept. 5, a local Black man who had assisted SNCC, Herbert Lee, was shot and killed by a white state representative who was never indicted. Several years later, a Black man who was witness to the shooting was beaten and later murdered. The McComb campaign was suspended.

By the Fall of 1961, there were 16 full-time SNCC "field secretaries," plus Executive Secretary James Forman, who were each paid a $40 per week salary. Under Forman, SNCC became more structured. In fact, if not officially it was moving from being a coordinating committee to becoming a cadre organization although that term was not used until much later.[5] At its next conference, in Atlanta in April 1962, SNCC reorganized. "SNCC's new structure," as Clayborne Carson describes it, "maintained the illusion that the primary function of the organization was to coordinate campus protest activities, whereas SNCC now existed mainly to support the efforts of ex-students who had become staff members."[6]

SNCC continued to work on a number of desegregation campaigns in the Deep South. That fall, SNCC went to Albany, Georgia, where nonviolent demonstrations at a bus terminal and other facilities soon led to the formation of a much wider coalition of groups called the Albany Movement. Waves of arrests in the hundreds, including on one occasion, Martin Luther King Jr. who had come to assist, came in the following months. Albany authorities appeared to be following a new strategy: "Arrest quickly, quietly, and imprison. Move before white mobs can form, avoid brutal actions which can mobilize national support."[7] The Albany Movement continued its pressure well into December and finally achieved results: desegregation of bus and train facilities and release of those imprisoned. What this actually meant was simply that in Albany, existing law would be carried out rather than defied.

In the surrounding counties, however, several Black churches were burned down. Shots were fired into homes where SNCC workers were staying. SNCC once again learned that beyond rhetoric, the federal government, in particular the FBI, was not to be trusted to intervene in any reliable manner on behalf of the law.

Elsewhere in the South local activists and SNCC workers were continually arrested, some SNCC people 20 or more times. In Southwest Georgia, the number of incidents of Blacks being attacked during demonstrations during 1962 and 1963 ran to eight single-spaced pages.[8] In February 1962, Charles McDew, who was then SNCC chairman, and two other SNCC workers were arrested in Baton Rouge, Louisiana, on criminal anarchy charges based on their membership in SNCC, which was accused of seeking the overthrow of the state government. McDew and Bob Zellner were jailed for 35 days in "sweatbox" cells that could well have killed them.[9] Zellner had already been convicted on similar charges during the Albany demonstrations and served a month on a Black "chain gang" repairing roads even though he was white. This did not endanger him since his affiliation with SNCC was well-known to the Black convicts.

In the Deep South repression precluded further progress to integrate public facilities. SNCC's strategic turn to voter registration and running Black candidates for public office was based on the thinking that although there was no chance of an electoral victory, a campaign would be able to publicize Black grievances. An initial publicity effort was the attempt to integrate the visitors' sections of both the Georgia and Mississippi state legislatures, which resulted in numerous arrests.

That spring several foundations provided funds for a Voter Education Project with the objective of registering Black people to support Democratic Party candidates. The theory was that the federal government would be forced to provide protection for people attempting to register to vote. This was the first step in an ongoing campaign that would focus national attention on the scandal of the exclusion of Blacks from full citizenship.

In the fall of 1962, A. Philip Randolph, the Black socialist labor leader, proposed a March on Washington to pressure the Kennedy administration to support legislation providing equal rights in employment, voting, and public accommodations. Randolph had initiated a March on Washington Movement in 1941 for a similar purpose, but it was called off after President Franklin D. Roosevelt enacted some equal employment reforms covering federal contracts in military production. The new March was planned for August 28, 1963. One of the speakers was SNCC's John Lewis. The original draft of his speech, which attacked the federal government and called for nonviolent revolution, was toned down after considerable pressure from other civil rights leaders. But he was able to keep that part calling for Backs to "stay in the streets until the unfinished revolution of 1776 is complete."[10] (A Civil Rights bill was passed on July 2, 1964, after 54 days of blockage by Southern senators, but only at the cost of significant compromises.)

Within SNCC's ranks, distrust of the federal government, based on many instances of the failure of federal agencies including the FBI to enforce existing laws, was spreading. Some SNCC workers were beginning to adopt more radical views. 1963 was marked by assassinations and bombings. According to Carson, 20,000 people were arrested during civil rights demonstrations in the South that year. Among those murdered were William Moore, a white civil rights activist, who was assassinated on April 20. Medgar

Evers, a NAACP leader in Mississippi, was shot down on June 12. A notorious local segregationist, Byron De La Beckwith, was charged but after two trials with all-white juries, no conviction was forthcoming. (In 1989 new evidence was produced, and Beckwith was finally convicted. He was sentenced to life imprisonment and died in prison in 2001).

On September 15, 1963, four girls aged 11-14 died in the bombing of a Black church in Birmingham, Alabama. Several SNCC leaders, despite their continuing skepticism, concluded that without intervention from Washington, the climate of terror in the Deep South would prevent any substantial changes in the segregationist system.

How was this intervention to be accomplished? By now a Council of Federated Organizations (COFO) including SNCC and several other groups had been formed in Mississippi, and the early stages of what was to become a massive campaign to register Black voters got underway. The first step was a state-wide "Freedom Ballot," a mock election that drew more than 80,000 Black "voters" to demonstrate Mississippi Blacks' desire to vote. The next step was the Mississippi Summer Project of 1964, better known as "Freedom Summer," which would include white Northern volunteers. This was a matter of some controversy then and later within SNCC, many of whose members feared that whites would take over and that many whites' attitudes were elitist so that they would not be able to relate to sharecroppers and farm laborers, SNCC's intended base of support. Also, in view of the miserable conditions in Mississippi's segregated Black public schools, SNCC planned to create "freedom schools" in which volunteers (mainly from the North) would, that Summer, teach Black youths in Mississippi subjects ranging from basic education to Black history and leadership skills. The Voter Registration Project was not accepted without considerable debate, but finally COFO, despite the lukewarm support of the NAACP and SCLC, gave its formal approval in January 1964. CORE, which supported the idea, was able to take on only one-fifth of the Project; it was pretty much SNCC's baby.

SNCC thought that since local and state authorities, supplemented by local mobs, would undoubtedly block any attempts to register Black voters, the federal government would be forced to enter the picture, whether the President liked it or not. America's image in world politics, in the midst of the Cold War, was, after all, at stake. To push this strategy further, a Mississippi Freedom Democratic Party, separate from the segregationist official Democratic Party, was created. The plan was to challenge the regular Democratic Party and attempt to displace it at the Party's August 1964 Presidential Convention in Atlantic City, New Jersey.

Meanwhile, even as planning proceeded, the Howard University (Washington, D.C.) Nonviolent Action Group (NAG), an SNCC affiliate, was diverted to Cambridge, Maryland to help with a demonstration against segregationist Governor George Wallace of Alabama, who was scheduled to speak at an all-white rally on May 11. The person who had initiated the idea was Gloria Richardson, a highly respected local Black leader. Cambridge is located on the agricultural Eastern Shore of Maryland, which at the time closely resembled the Deep

South in terms of "race relations." When about 600 people began to march towards the Wallace rally, the Maryland National Guard, which was already policing the Black community, quickly appeared and blocked them. Richardson and several others moved forward and were arrested. The remaining Black marchers were then dispersed with a gas attack. Cleveland Sellers, who was gassed and arrested shortly later, claims it was nauseating, not tear, gas, and that Guardsmen were also firing live ammunition. In the subsequent confusion, some Black men began to shoot at the Guardsmen in order to stop them from further attacking the fleeing demonstrators.[11]

In mid-June, 1964, some 300 college students, mostly white Northerners, were brought to a college in Oxford, Ohio, to prepare for the COFO voter registration campaign. A similar group was brought for the Freedom School project. Overall about 900 volunteers eventually participated, of whom about 135 were Black.

At the training sessions, a representative of the U.S. Justice Department, John Doar, told the volunteers that the federal government could only investigate incidents, it could not protect voter registration workers. He said protection was up to local police, which the volunteers knew meant the opposite, since local police in Mississippi were collaborators, if not actual perpetrators, of outrages against civil rights activists. The volunteers were shocked. But Doar's statement was patently untrue. Two years earlier President Kennedy had sent federal troops to protect James Meredith as he attempted to register as a student at the segregated University of Mississippi. Moreover, there are numerous federal laws

23

that could have been invoked by Lyndon Johnson, who became president after the assassination of Kennedy in November 1963.[12]

Then, three volunteers including two CORE workers (James Chaney, Black, and Michael Schwerner, white) and one fresh from the Oxford orientation (Andrew Goodman, white), disappeared after having been briefly arrested in Philadelphia, Mississippi. A Black church, the Mt. Zion United Methodist, near Philadelphia, had been burned to the ground. The church had hosted civil rights meetings and had agreed to sponsor a Freedom School. The three men left to investigate on June 21. Their bodies were found on August 4. During the search, the bodies of three other Black men, one wearing a CORE T-shirt, were also found. The record is clear that the FBI was notified immediately when the men went missing but took no action in the critical two days between the disappearance and the murders. The FBI in Mississippi at that time was all-white, and most were native to the state.[13]

On December 4, 1964, 21 men were arrested by the FBI for violating the civil rights of the victims (since the state had refused to indict them for murder or anything else). A few days later a U.S. Commissioner dropped the charges based on the fact that the FBI's testimony was second-hand and there were no actual witnesses willing to testify. Two years later the U.S. Department of Justice charged 18 men with violating the civil rights of the victims. These included the Sheriff, Lawrence Rainey, the Deputy Sheriff, Cecil Price, and a Baptist minister, Edgar Ray Killen. Seven, including Price, were found guilty by an all-white jury and served sentences of up to six years. Rainey and Killen were freed. In 2005 Killen was retried by the State of Mississippi after new evidence was uncovered, and he was convicted of the three murders and sentenced to 20 years for each. He was 80 at the time.

The project, including the Freedom Schools, went forward, despite continuing attacks, including bombings, many assaults, and about 1,000 arrests. COFO collected data about these events that went to 26 pages.[14] That there was not even more violence was attributed by a number of participants to the fact that Black farmers in the areas where organizing was going on were armed. Also, there was widespread press coverage. Although the actual number of Blacks who managed to register to vote was modest, the project did generate a great deal of publicity and certainly deepened the political awareness of both Black and white volunteers and their Freedom School students. In Biloxi, SNCC initiated a White Community Pilot Project in an attempt to get support from poor whites for the Mississippi Freedom Democratic Party. The SNCC teams were integrated. One white recruited by the Project served as a delegate to the Atlantic City, N.J. Democratic Presidential Convention later that year.[15] Although this was somewhat of a breakthrough, and a revelation to some of the whites who were visited in their homes by these integrated teams, within the larger Project tensions between Black and white volunteers contributed significantly to SNCC's gradual move away from being an interracial organization.

The Mississippi Freedom Democratic Party delegation to the Democratic Party Convention that

25

August included a number of SNCC members. At first, it seemed that its challenge to be seated in place of the segregationist official Democratic Party might work, especially after testimony before the Party's Credentials Committee by Mississippian Fannie Lou Hamer, who had been beaten in jail following her arrest during the voter registration campaign. However, the MFDP faced the formidable obstacle that a number of their liberal and labor union allies favored a compromise, backed by the Johnson administration. President Johnson and his vice-presidential nominee-to-be, Senator Hubert Humphrey, were afraid that support for the MFDP would alienate Southern whites, who up to that time still generally supported the Democratic Party. Another factor was the fear of a victory by the Republican candidate, Barry Goldwater, who was not only deeply conservative but very much a saber-rattling super-patriot. Many Democrats thought if he were elected, he would be prepared to pull the nuclear trigger against the Soviet Union. Thus every effort had to be made to keep the Southern Democrats in the Johnson fold, which meant keeping the MFDP out. Johnson's people used every tactic in the book of rotten politics to persuade the members of the Credentials Committee not to seat the MFDP. Members were promised jobs; others were threatened with taking jobs away. Even Martin Luther King Jr. was persuaded to back the compromise.

It would have allowed the MFDP only two seats, and not as delegates from Mississippi but as at-large delegates picked by the Party. The compromise was rejected by the MFDP delegates. They attempted to take seats but were hustled out. They went home, many of the SNCC delegates feeling that working within the conventional political system was useless. "In the eyes of the SNCC leadership, the Northern liberal elite had finally shown its true colors; moral force had proven no match for raw political power."[16] "Never again," Cleveland Sellers wrote later, "were we lulled into believing that our task was exposing injustices so that the 'good' people of America could eliminate them. After Atlantic City, our struggle was not for civil rights, but for liberation."[17]

Ironically, the official Mississippi delegation declared it would not support Johnson anyway, and the majority of whites in Mississippi voted for Barry Goldwater, the Senator from Arizona. He won Mississippi that November, but lost the election to Johnson. He carried only his own state, plus all of the states of the Deep South: South Carolina, Georgia, Alabama, Mississippi, and Louisiana. Four years later a third-party segregationist George Wallace, Governor of Alabama, carried these same states, minus South Carolina, plus Arkansas. The South was lost to the Democratic Party.

Chapter 3
From Freedom Now to Black Power

*"We been saying freedom for six years and we aren't
got nothing. What we going to start saying now is Black
Power!"[1]*

It had become clear to many in SNCC after the
murders of Chaney, Goodman, and Schwerner in July
1964, during Freedom Summer that the federal
government would not intervene even to protect white
volunteers, much less Blacks. The issue of armed defense
was now on the agenda. The question had come up at the
Atlanta staff meeting the previous June, where those who
were skeptical about white volunteers coming to the
project also advocated that SNCC workers be allowed to
arm themselves.[2] The decision at that time was that no
guns were to be kept in any SNCC facility and that SNCC
staff were not to carry guns. But SNCC refrained from
taking a public stand on armed self-defense for others. A
succession of CORE conventions going back to 1962
also debated the question, with James Farmer, CORE's
national director at the time, an old-time advocate of
nonviolence, expressing fear that white liberal support
would be undermined if Southern activists became
openly violent even in self-defense. Nevertheless, Black
farmers who provided safe houses for volunteers were
often armed and in a number of communities had
organized armed patrols to protect themselves against
white vigilantes long before the summer of 1964.
According to Akinyele Umoja, who conducted many
interviews with SNCC veterans, Stokely Carmichael,
who would later be SNCC chairman, remembers the
famous MFDP leader and spokesperson in Atlantic City

Fanny Lou Hamer handing him a revolver while he was staying at her home in Ruleville, Mississippi.

That fall, after most of the Northern white volunteers had gone home, the Ku Klux Klan and local police increased their level of harassment and violence against the continuing voting rights campaign. In McComb, Mississippi, Black residents reacted to a bombing on September 20 by coming into the streets armed with guns, Molotov cocktails, and other weapons, and attacking whites and white establishments. Finally, the federal government reacted. Nine Klansmen were tried for arson and bombing in October. After pleading guilty, they were put on probation.

By this time it was clear that SNCC's relations with other civil rights groups and with liberal and labor supporters had deteriorated. SNCC's criticism of the government at the March on Washington in August 1963 was the first open break. The MFDP's refusal to compromise in Atlantic City was another factor. But strains had also developed during the run-up to Freedom Summer when SNCC refused to sever ties to the National Lawyers Guild, which was providing legal counsel in a number of SNCC cases. The NLG was considered by mainstream civil rights and liberal groups to be Communist-influenced. SNCC's staff now numbered 200 and was scattered over four states organizing for voting rights and operating Freedom Schools. SNCC had become the face of civil rights, to the chagrin of some of the older, established organizations. They feared that SNCC's radical turn would reflect badly on them.

The consequence of all these factors was that funds were drying up. It was not clear that there had been much progress on voting rights. Morale was down. A reassessment was called for. It would be influenced by the experience of several SNCC leaders who had gone to Africa in September as part of a larger delegation sponsored by Harry Belafonte. There they were exposed to the socialist ideas of Sekou Touré, the President of Guinea. Several of the group went on to tour other African countries. They also met with Malcolm X, who was in Kenya at the time. This was the beginning of a relationship that would last until Malcolm X's assassination on Feb. 21, 1965. The contact with Malcolm X worried mainstream civil rights leaders.

In mid-November, 1964, SNCC staff met at Waveland, Mississippi to reevaluate strategy. A Molotov cocktail was thrown. Some of the SNCC staff were armed and rushed after the perpetrators, who were caught, warned, and released. Howard Zinn, the radical history professor who was the first to publish a study of SNCC,[3] was told by a participant, "You have just witnessed the end of the nonviolent movement."[4]

The meeting lasted seven days. James Forman, an advocate of a more centralized and disciplined organization proposed that SNCC's structure move in the direction of control being in the hands of the staff rather than that of the representatives of various student groups. "This recommendation acknowledged that the group was no longer a coordinating body for campus-based organizations but instead a group of professional organizers."[5] However, this issue, as well as others, remained unsettled at the close of the week.

Meanwhile, strains between white and Black staff were increasing. The latter feared that the increase in white staff would inhibit the development of local Black leaders. This "foreshadowed a new racial consciousness that would pervade the Black struggle in the last half of the decade."[6]

Controversy swirled around a demand from a women's workshop that SNCC deal with discrimination against the women in its ranks. A group of women presented a position paper, "Women in the Movement," which charged that women were mostly assigned to office tasks whereas some SNCC veterans, both men and women, pointed to the important positions held by women, such as Fanny Lou Hamer and Diane Nash. Howard University student Muriel Tillinghast became Project Director in Greenville, Mississippi after only a month in the field during Freedom Summer. SNCC's women have testified on both sides of the issue. Jean Smith Young, also a Howard University student participating in Freedom Summer, for example, stated that she "never felt discriminated against as a woman felt and experienced quite the opposite. SNCC was a liberating experience for me as a woman."[7] Stokely Carmichael's notorious remark made apparently in jest, that the position of women in SNCC was "prone," on the other hand, didn't help dispel the idea that there was at least some truth to the discrimination story. During Freedom Summer, according to a careful analysis by Doug McAdam, women were more likely to be assigned teaching and clerical roles. Partly this was due to the staff's feeling that having white women in the field canvassing door to door would endanger not only themselves but also jeopardize the success of the project since it would be extremely threatening to the white community and would trigger more violence. "The net effect of this policy was to reproduce traditional sex and work roles"[8]

More important, perhaps, was the highly charged and divisive role of sexual relations among the Freedom Summer volunteers, and in SNCC more generally. "There was a point," Michael Simmons reported, "when every major Black figure in SNCC had a white girlfriend."[9] During Freedom Summer white female volunteers faced an "explosive" dilemma: "They could either reject Black males' advances and risk being labeled a racist, or they could go along at considerable physical and psychological cost to themselves."[10] Demonstrating another dimension of this double standard, Black women volunteers who dated white male volunteers faced SNCC staff tongue lashings; Black men who dated white women did not.

Adding to SNCC's difficulties were resentments between the more "middle-class" staff, both Black and white, and Black staff who came out of local struggles and were less formally educated. James Forman, the veteran Executive Secretary, also felt that Northern "middle class" elements were spreading the use of marijuana, which he considered politically dangerous.

A considerable amount of disorganization followed the Waveland retreat. The Mississippi Freedom Democratic Party supported Lyndon Johnson in November 1964, to the dismay of most SNCC staff. The Voting Rights Act of 1965 was on the horizon, and the MFDP had been promised seats at the 1968 Democratic

Convention. Participation in the two-party system was becoming more feasible at least in some parts of the Deep South, especially in urban areas. SNCC, however, was turning in the opposite direction, towards more radical views.

In January 1965, SNCC challenged the seating of Jamie L. Whitten and four others who had been elected to the House of Representatives from Mississippi the previous November on the basis that Blacks were excluded from voting. The House voted 228-143 to seat them nevertheless. Actually, although having 143 Representatives voting to support the challenge was a pretty good outcome, the objective of the challenge was "to prove that the system would not work for poor Black people."[11] Yet Sellers and his colleagues would be proven wrong within a few years.

Early in 1965 Martin Luther King Jr. and the Southern Christian Leadership Conference initiated a voting rights campaign in Selma, Alabama, the county seat of Dallas County, which was then more than half Black, with only 130 registered to vote out of some 15,000 Black adults. Nearby, neither Lowndes nor Wilcox Counties had a single Black voter. SNCC felt that the campaign, centered on King, would inhibit efforts to develop local leadership, and that "local Blacks would have little to show for their sacrifices when SCLC's entourage left town."[12] King was arrested on February 1 in Selma, setting off marches that led to a thousand more arrests, including hundreds of school children. With some reluctance, SNCC joined the campaign.

In March, following the shooting of Black protester Jimmy Lee Jackson by a state policeman, the SCLC decided on a march from Selma to Montgomery to publicize the disastrous conditions facing Blacks in Alabama. About 2,000 began the march on March 7. SNCC did not participate officially, but many individuals, including SNCC chairman John Lewis, did. At the Pettus Bridge just outside Selma, the marchers were ordered to disperse and when they did not, the police attacked, using clubs and tear gas. There were many injuries. Lewis was hospitalized with a fractured skull. SNCC workers from several states immediately descended on Selma. The march resumed a few days later only to be halted by police again. Martin Luther King, at the head of the march, then turned it around in order to avoid further violence. During the following days, three white clergy who supported the movement were attacked by local white thugs. One, James Reeb, died of his injuries. In contrast to the shooting of Jackson, this incident created a public uproar. The march finally did continue to Montgomery, accompanied by U.S. Army and Alabama National Guard troops. On March 25, after a rally at the capital, Viola Liuzzo, a white volunteer who was driving to Montgomery, was killed by a sniper. [13]

President Johnson used the Selma incidents to advocate new federal voter legislation. After the passage of the 1964 Civil Rights Act, he realized that the Democratic Party was finished as far as the South was concerned and that it would not make a comeback until Black people voted in much larger numbers. (Indeed, the DP has not yet fully recovered from even Johnson's far-from-radical civil rights policies. While Jimmy Carter did carry the South for the Party in 1976, it was not until

32 years later, when Barack Obama won the Presidency in 2008, before the Party was able to make inroads in the South. Yet Obama carried only the Southern states of Florida, North Carolina, and Virginia. Most whites in the South continue to vote against the party that is viewed by many of them, right or wrong, consciously or not, as the "Black party." In fact, the higher the percentage of Black voters in a Southern state, the lower the percentage of whites voting for the Democratic Party.)

Following the Selma demonstrations, Stokely Carmichael, a veteran SNCC organizer, moved to Lowndes County, Alabama, to lead the campaign to register Black voters. In August, a federal voting registrar arrived and registration became somewhat easier, despite arrests and one shooting. Given the impossibility of taking over the segregationist Democratic Party organization, it was decided to organize a third party, the Lowndes County Freedom Organization. It used the ballot symbol of a Black Panther, in contrast to the white rooster of the official Democratic Party. Soon the name would be changed to the Black Panther Party (not to be confused with the Black Panther Party in California, which also adopted the symbol). It was an all-Black party simply because no local white would join. Carmichael told prospective members that the role of the Party was just like that of other parties: "We want power, that's all we want."[14] Most local Black farmers were armed; so were many SNCC workers in Lowndes County. In addition, the Deacons for Defense and Justice, a Louisiana group consisting mostly of Black military veterans, occasionally provided guards at Black gatherings.

The strategy in Georgia was different. Julian Bond, SNCC's communications director and one of its founders, won a seat in the Georgia State House of Representatives running as a Democrat. While not all SNCC workers supported this strategy, most in Atlanta SNCC worked hard on the campaign. He was refused the seat by the white legislators due to his support for SNCC and its opposition to the Vietnam War. The U.S. Supreme Court later ordered him seated. And he later won a seat in the U.S. House of Representatives. By that time Bond had distanced himself from SNCC, feeling that its radical reputation would undermine his electoral chances.

The 1964 and 1965 Civil Rights and Voting Rights Acts and President Johnson's anti-poverty programs now presented SNCC with the classic dilemma of which direction to take. The reformist path seemed increasingly attractive to many since voter registration and electoral successes were now on the horizon. Also, the Economic Opportunity Act of 1964, the so-called "War on Poverty," seemed to create real opportunities to change communities, and real salaries with which to support families. Many SNCC staff, however, rejected these strategies as inadequate and cooptative. James Forman had predicted Washington's strategy and its consequences: The government "would pay people to work in its poverty programs—a reformist trap designed to militate against basic changes, for the government is not about to finance programs that are working to destroy the present economic and political system."[15]

The year following Freedom Summer marked the high point of SNCC's strength. By the summer of 1965, there were 200 full-time SNCC workers. However, this

36

very growth also opened the organization to more factionalism. Essentially the argument was between a group referred to as "freedom high," meaning a tendency to behave on the basis of individual conscience and somewhat of a lack of organizational discipline, versus a "hard-liner" group that favored a more disciplined approach. This faction was at the same time moving in a Black Nationalist direction.[16]

Black Nationalist tendencies within SNCC, influenced by Malcolm X and others, obviously led to white SNCC staff feeling increasingly unwelcome. At the Kingston Springs, Tennessee staff meeting in May 1966, Stokeley Carmichael, who was much more inclined towards Black Nationalism and was increasingly dubious about nonviolence, replaced John Lewis as chairperson. Carmichael was 24 years old. Lewis was seen as insufficiently militant and too close to mainstream civil rights groups, especially the religiously oriented SCLC. The issue of whites in SNCC now became urgent. If SNCC was 25% white, how could it develop a "Black consciousness?" Sellers asked later.

The Kerkonson, New York staff meeting in December 1966, was the last one with any white staff. By this time almost all whites had left, either to organize among Southern whites or, since that was difficult, to say the least, to move into other political arenas, specifically the anti-war movement. SNCC's going all-Black contributed further to its abandonment by the white liberal and mainstream civil rights community.

The Vietnam War had by this point become perhaps the country's major political issue. After the shooting of

SNCC volunteer Sammy Younge, a U.S. Navy veteran, on Jan. 3, 1966, as he tried to integrate a "white" bathroom in Tuskegee, Alabama, the SNCC Executive Committee not only voted to oppose the U.S. government's foreign policy but went so far as to advocate support for draft resisters. This resulted in SNCC's further isolation from mainstream civil rights organizations that were loyal to the Johnson administration.

SNCC's move in the direction of Black Nationalism gained ground with a resurgence of protests following the shooting of James Meredith on June 5, 1966. In 1962 Meredith had been the first Black to attend the University of Mississippi. His successful effort to enroll required the use of 31,000 troops including 11,000 Mississippi National Guardsmen called into federal service, plus a contingent of U.S. Marshalls, to put down what amounted to an armed insurrection by white citizens from across the state protesting integration of "Ole' Miss." This was three times the number of U.S. soldiers in West Berlin at the time. Ironically, an order from Washington forbade direct participation by Black soldiers from units of the 82nd and 101st Airborne Divisions despite protests from their officers.[17]

On June 5, 1966, Meredith decided to walk from Memphis, Tennessee, to Jackson, Mississippi to promote voter registration. A day later he was shot and wounded by a sniper. SNCC, CORE, and King decided to continue the march and utilize it to register Black voters along the route. Willie Ricks, an SNCC field organizer, at this point, proposed using the slogan of Black Power to arouse local Blacks to join the campaign. It was quickly supported by James Forman back in Atlanta, and Carmichael who was with the march. Carmichael wanted to de-emphasize white participation and supported the inclusion of the armed Deacons group. King was dismayed, feeling that the slogan would backfire, alienate white supporters, and provide ammunition to racists. Even Meredith opposed the slogan. The NAACP and the Urban League, another old-line mainstream civil rights group, both withdrew from the march. John Lewis was similarly critical, and in a later interview termed the slogan "meaningless rhetoric." Vice-President Hubert Humphrey spoke out against it. Yet it was supported in the form of a full-page advertisement in *The New York Times* by the National Committee of Negro Churchmen.

Carmichael was arrested on June 17, then released and at a rally in Greenwood, Mississippi, deliberately made a point of raising the slogan of Black Power. The march ended in Jackson, Mississippi, after it had been attacked by white mobs and police at two earlier points. In Jackson Carmichael again raised the slogan of Black Power. The problem was that the slogan could be, and was, interpreted in many ways. The mainstream media took it as promoting violence and hatred of whites, even as "reverse racism." The NAACP swiftly condemned it because it seemed separatist, that is, opposed to integration. Soon mainstream civil rights groups and leaders, including Congressman Adam Clayton Powell from Harlem, maneuvered to co-opt the slogan, even holding several "Black Power" conferences. It was used by some Black leaders as rhetoric to promote Black business entrepreneurship. Yet Carmichael initially advocated only building a Black political base in order to elect Black people to public office. Later, in 1967, he wrote, with political scientist Charles V. Hamilton, *Black Power, the Politics of Liberation in America.* Here the authors adopt a clearly radical, quasi-Marxist Black nationalist theory, that "Black people in this country form a colony they stand as colonial subjects in relation to white society."[18] Regardless of interpretation, however, it galvanized young Blacks and its militant tone seemed to revive a sense of organizing possibilities. But it also irreparably sundered the tenuous coalition of civil rights forces in which up to now SNCC had played perhaps the leading role. [See Appendix C.]

Chapter 4
Many Ways to Die

Ira Grupper, a young, white SNCC staff member, paid a visit to a man named Vernon Dahmer sometime in the spring of 1965. Dahmer, a Black businessman, was the head of the Hattiesburg, Mississippi NAACP. Nailed to a tree in Dahmer's yard was a KKK flier in the format of a traditional armed forces recruiting poster, featuring the well-known "Uncle Sam" altered to look like a Klansman. It said, "I want you in the White Knights of Mississippi Ku Klux Klan." Dahmer tore the flier off the tree and gave it to Grupper as a souvenir. The following January, after an apprehensive Dahmer had sent his family away, his house was firebombed and he was killed.

Meanwhile a new front had opened in U.S. race history. Northern urban "ghettos," beginning in Harlem, New York City, on July 18, 1964, exploded into a series of "race riots." These continued year after year, mostly in the summer months, mainly in Northern cities, with increasing violence until local, state, and the federal authorities responded with overwhelming force. In Philadelphia, Pennsylvania a riot involving Black citizens exploded on August 28. For three days white-owned businesses in the predominantly Black section of North Philadelphia were looted and police were attacked. Two people were killed and many injured, including 100 police.[1] In the Watts section of Los Angeles, California, in August 1965, 4,000 people were arrested, 34 killed, and about $35 million in damage resulted from nearly two days of rioting. In the Newark, New Jersey riot of July 12-17, 1967, the National Guard was called out. 23 people were killed. In Detroit a week later, 5,000 National Guardsmen were called in to control rioting. Following the assassination of Martin Luther King Jr. in the Spring of 1968, riots broke out in 138 cities. About 60,000 soldiers were called out to suppress them. More than 40 Black people were killed and some 20,000 were arrested at least briefly. These riots, termed "insurrections" by some, were not white versus Black. They were mainly attacks against property; property not owned by Blacks. The context, as President Johnson clearly understood, was the conditions prevalent in the decaying centers of cities that had become predominantly Black after World War II, with high rates of poverty and unemployment, job discrimination, poor educational facilities, and police hostility particularly against Black youth. Trigger incidents often involved an altercation with police. In urban areas progress towards equal opportunity was miniscule, and the tactics of nonviolence were difficult to employ against landlords and politicians who were some distance removed. The riots continued despite the passage of the Economic Opportunity Act of 1964, which provided significant sums to create programs to assist unemployed youth (including whites) and promoted "maximum feasible participation of residents" in local employment and other improvement programs.[2]

Quickly the more militant civil rights organizations, such as CORE and SNCC, began "a veritable northward stampede to establish organizational footholds in the ghetto" Understandably, given the usual internal disputes and difficulties in relating to a population in the urban North that was very different from the rural South, this was a tough job. Yet Jacobs and Landau's view that "the masses of poor Negroes remain an unorganized minority in swelling urban ghettos, and neither SNCC nor any other group has found a form of political organization that can convert the energy of the slums into political power"[3] is an exaggeration, as events in Philadelphia, to use only one example, will show.

It is a mistake to think of CORE and SNCC as entering a political vacuum. CORE already had chapters in a number of Northern cities. Political organizations of several tendencies, Black, white, Latinx, and sometimes a combination of all of the above existed in many urban areas. In Philadelphia a "Freedom Library" bookstore organized by a former SNCC worker led to the formation of the Black People's Unity Movement, a Black Nationalist group with connections to an activist Black Episcopalian (Anglican) Church. In the Spring and Summer of 1966, there were numerous Black Power rallies, including one at which Stokely Carmichael spoke. Early in 1967, following demonstrations by Black public school students demanding curriculum reforms, a riot involving police brutality led to the formation of People for Human Rights. The organizers were white New Left activists who had founded a project to tutor poor, mainly Black, students. There was a chapter of the National Welfare Rights Organization, mostly Black women who were receiving stipends under the Aid to Dependent Children program. There was a local wing of the Black Economic Development Conference, James Forman's project. There was a militant NAACP chapter. There were other social services and anti-poverty groups oriented to Black community issues. Soon, the Black Panther Party would also appear. In brief, as in most other cities, the North Philadelphia "ghetto" was far from the stereotype of a disorganized, anomic mass, into which SNCC or other groups could simply move in. Yet despite this infrastructure, the North Philadelphia "ghetto" also had the appearance of an "internal colony" as theorized by Carmichael and Hamilton.

In Chicago, Illinois, to cite yet another example, Jobs or Income Now (JOIN), an outgrowth of Students for a Democratic Society's community organizing project, was formed in 1964 to organize poor whites. A leading figure was Peggy Terry, a white woman who had worked with Chicago CORE. One objective was to align with other organizations, including the Panthers, the Young Lords (a former Puerto Rican street gang), the Young Patriots Organization (poor whites emigrated from the South) and others to form what eventually became the Rainbow Coalition in 1969.

In Philadelphia, SNCC shifted its focus from being a support group for SNCC in the South to community organizing. In late 1965 it sponsored a Philadelphia Freedom Organization patterned after the Lowndes County Freedom Organization. However, this ran head-on against the almost hegemonic role of the NAACP and its charismatic leader, Cecil Moore, as well as challenging the local Democratic Party's influence over the Black vote. Even more critical was the determination of the police department, under Frank Rizzo (who would soon become Mayor) to crush radical Black activity. The SNCC office was under constant surveillance.[4]

On August 13, 1966, some 80 police supported by a force of a thousand more raided the SNCC office, the Freedom Library, and two residences housing local

44

militants. Four people including one SNCC staff worker were arrested and charged with possession of dynamite. Eventually, the charges were dropped, but SNCC's efforts in Philadelphia came to a halt. In Chicago, the SNCC office was also targeted by the police. SNCC's lead organizer there left for exile in Tanzania. In Atlanta, after a riot broke out following a police shooting, Carmichael and several other SNCC workers were arrested and charged with inciting a riot. Their convictions were later overturned on appeal. James Forman concluded that "the total power structure of the United States was out to destroy SNCC."[5] SNCC's top leadership warned the staff: "We feel there is a growing trend of 'plants', frames, indictments, and other attacks, intended to completely destroy the organization."[6]

A political backlash to the urban uprisings (and the increasing militancy of students, symbolized by the Berkeley Free Speech Movement of September, 1964-January, 1965) was setting in. Black support for Democratic candidates for public office led to a Republican strategy to use "law and order" and patriotic, pro-war rhetoric to sway white Democrats to the Republican side. Moreover, the riots led to massive expenditures by local governments to provide their police forces with the latest weaponry, even including tanks in some cities. The FBI engaged in successful efforts to infiltrate and undermine not only radical Black organizations but even more moderate civil rights groups. Bob Zellner believed that both Black and white informers, including *agents provocateurs*, had been in SNCC from the beginning. Official documents recently disclosed that from 1964 a vice-president of Mississippi's NAACP worked as an informer for an

45

agency hired by the state's "Sovereignty Commission," a kind of state FBI, to spy on civil rights activists.

SNCC's main efforts, however, remained focused on the South. Early in 1967 conflicts between SNCC's Atlanta Project staff and the National Office came to a head. Stokely Carmichael called the Atlanta police to report an automobile in possession of the Atlanta Project as missing, which led the Atlanta group to attack James Forman, who was Carmichael's backer, for descending "to the level of calling a racist henchman cop of the white master (Mayor) Allen to settle an internal dispute." Calling the police had long been taboo. Internal dissension, resentment about Carmichael's "star" status, and attacks not only by mainstream civil rights groups but even more importantly by various police entities including the F.B.I.'s COINTELPRO continued to weaken the organization.[7] A year later, Sellers recalled, there were only ten SNCC offices in operation.

Following a talk by Carmichael at Vanderbilt University in Nashville, Tennessee April 8, 1967, an incident, again involving the police, triggered a riot. Police riot squads fired, hitting a building at the nearby black Fisk University and injuring several students. SNCC was blamed for the riot, and its offices in Nashville were raided. Several SNCC workers were arrested. At Texas Southern University in Houston, university officials prohibited the formation of a "Friends of SNCC" chapter. In May, during a mass student demonstration protesting this prohibition, police fired into dormitories, invaded and vandalized rooms, and arrested 481 people.

By the Spring of 1967, as the Vietnam War intensified, 16 SNCC staff had been drafted into the armed forces. Most refused induction; one, Cleveland Sellers, SNCC's Program Secretary, was indicted and later served the five-year maximum. Another, Michael Simmons, served two years. At a huge anti-war "mobilization" in New York City on April 15, under the watchful eyes of the FBI, Carmichael, Rev. King, Dr. Benjamin Spock, Harry Belafonte, and several others linked arms to lead off the march. SNCC provided marshals. Upwards of 125,000 participated.

Carmichael's militantly anti-war and Black Power speeches had attracted too much negative attention. At a staff meeting in Atlanta in May, he stepped down and was replaced as chairman by H. "Rap" Brown, who had been organizing in Alabama. Since Sellers was now out of the picture, Ralph Featherstone replaced him as Program Secretary. The meeting lasted two days, during which Bob Zellner, the white Alabaman who had been de facto expelled the previous December, made a proposal that he and his wife Dorothy work in the white community under SNCC's sponsorship. This fell through because Zellner would not accept the "second-class citizenship" of not being allowed full staff membership. The previous vote to revoke membership for all whites was reaffirmed after considerable acrimonious debate. The Zellners continued their organizing project on their own.

"Rap" Brown strongly supported the right to armed self-defense and he often carried a weapon. He had an arrest record for carrying a concealed weapon. He was quoted as saying "If America chooses to play Nazi, Black

47

folks ain't going to play Jews."[8] Following a speech at an anti-Klan rally in Cambridge, Maryland, a riot broke out, the National Guard was sent by Governor Spiro Agnew (who later would be Richard Nixon's vice-president), and Brown was arrested for arson. Days later, he faced another gun charge. By June, "organizational disintegration (was) already far advanced. Only about seventy SNCC staff members remained." Leading figures including Diane Nash, John Lewis, and Bob Moses, had departed, and the joke was that "every word in SNCC's storied name was now a misnomer. They were no longer students or nonviolent. They no longer coordinated" anything.[9] The government's two-pronged strategy was becoming clear: repression on the one hand, but active recruitment by anti-poverty programs on the other, although top leaders who had become notorious were excluded. The FBI insisted that communists of varying tendencies had participated in, or influenced, SNCC actions. SNCC's connections to the National Lawyers Guild and the Southern Conference Educational Fund, both of which had "fellow traveler" reputations, were also used to smear SNCC, as was its anti-war draft resistance stance. SNCC's newsletter of June-July 1966 had run an article sympathetic to the Palestinian cause despite warnings from Forman and others that it would alienate many Jewish supporters and lead to charges of antisemitism, which in fact it did.

Meanwhile in Oakland, California, a new Black Power organization, the Black Panther Party for Self-Defense, had been created. (The Self-Defense part of the label was soon discarded.) It borrowed the symbol of the Black Panther from Alabama's Lowndes County Freedom Organization. Its defining characteristic, certainly in the minds of both Black and white Americans, was that it advocated armed self-defense. It sent armed squads to monitor the behavior of the Oakland police, and on May 2, 1967, it sent a unit including 20 armed men led by Panther founder Bobby Seale to the State Capitol in Sacramento to protest gun control legislation, a real irony since anti-gun control organizations were, and are, almost unanimously right-wing and tacitly if not overtly racist. A number of the Panthers were arrested but later released. The Panthers were now in the national press. SNCC and the Panthers quickly established a relationship; Huey P. Newton of the Panthers even asked Stokely Carmichael to serve as the Panthers' "field marshal" for the Eastern United States.

In September 1967 a National Conference for a New Politics, organized by mostly white leftist groups, failed to secure the allegiance of Black delegates despite winning virtually all of their demands, including 50% representation on all important committees. The strategy of inter-racial coalitions was dead as far as SNCC and other organizations identified with Black Power including the Panthers, were concerned. Even SNCC's draft resistance efforts, in the form of its National Black Anti-War Anti-Draft Union, were separate from the wider anti-war movement. Blacks at the famous Pentagon demonstration in October 1967, stayed away from the confrontations between white demonstrators, who faced 2500 federal troops, many with fixed bayonets, numerous U.S. Marshals, and clouds of tear gas.

However, the alternative strategy of unifying Black Power organizations would also fail. There were conflicting ideas about basic philosophy between the Panthers and SNCC and within SNCC itself. Ultimately these would prevent a merger between them. And there were serious conflicts between both and other Black organizations, especially the "US" organization of Ron "Maulana" Karenga, which was more oriented to the idea of a cultural "return to Africa" (spiritual, rather than literal) rather than to economic or political issues. On January 17, 1969, a conflict between the Panthers and the US over leadership of the University of California (Los Angeles) student government ended in a shootout and the deaths of two Panthers. There were violent clashes between the Panthers and the "US" in other parts of the country over the next several years.

Within SNCC, the argument was between those like Carmichael who saw "the problem" as primarily one of racial oppression, and those like Forman who believed the underlying issue was social class. Carmichael's advocacy of separatism and his rejection of "white" communism and socialism dismayed the Panthers, who, albeit an all-Black organization, accepted white support and also advocated a class approach, though it was to the "lumpenproletariat" rather than to the classic working class. Nevertheless, several SNCC members, including Carmichael himself, actually joined the Panthers briefly, and Forman allowed himself to be "drafted" as the Panthers' "minister of foreign affairs." He represented both SNCC and the Panthers at a conference in Sweden in April 1968 that included the National Liberation Front of Vietnam. He resigned from the Party in July, however, because he thought the Panthers were overly vulnerable to infiltration, and because of its inefficient administrative apparatus and lack of discipline. Yet he also saw the Panthers as authoritarian.[10] In July 1968, a planned joint SNCC-Panther rally at the United Nations in New York City collapsed due to friction between some SNCC staff and the Panther leadership. Carmichael remained a Panther, and SNCC expelled him.

Police repression of the Panthers, escalating in the Spring of 1968, became worse in the following years. There were a number of police raids, shootouts, and endless arrests and trials. In April 1968, Panther Bobby Hutton, a teenager, was killed during a shootout with Oakland police, even as he was surrendering, and Eldridge Cleaver was wounded. The Chicago police killed Panthers Fred Hampton (asleep and apparently drugged at the time) and Mark Clark during a raid on Dec. 4, 1969. Bobby Seale was constantly on trial: as part of the "Chicago Eight" following the Chicago Democratic Party Convention melee (see below), and in 1970 as one of the "New Haven 14" charged with the murder of an alleged police informer. From March 1968 to December 1969, 19 Panthers and sympathizers working with them were killed. COINTELPRO operations by the FBI, including fake threats by the Panthers to murder Forman and Carmichael, tried to exploit the differences between SNCC and the Panthers. The Philadelphia Panthers suffered constant police harassment and in August 1969, Panther offices were raided. Matthew J. Countryman summarizes: "As in other cities, the Philadelphia police seem to have taken the Panthers' talk of armed self-defense as a direct challenge." The police chief (Frank Rizzo) warned that "armed revolutionaries were invading the city."[11] By 1973 the Panthers had disappeared from the Philadelphia scene.

In February 1968, Rap Brown was arrested for violating bail conditions by flying to California to a rally in support of the imprisoned Panther Huey P. Newton. He was later sentenced to five years for transporting a rifle. By late 1968 Brown was facing fourteen criminal charges. Phil Hutchins, who succeeded Brown as chairman, faced charges in St. Louis, Missouri. Carmichael was under indictment for an Atlanta demonstration. "The government was on the offensive and everyone who had taken a revolutionary leadership position seemed to be fair game." [12] Then, at South Carolina State College in Orangeburg, after a series of demonstrations about university policy, and then focusing on segregated facilities in the downtown area, police backed by the National Guard occupied the campus. Believing that a shot had been fired at a police officer, police fired on students. 33 demonstrators were shot by police. Three died, in what became known as the Orangeburg Massacre. Again, SNCC was blamed. Rev. King demanded that the U.S. Justice Department take action to prosecute the police but FBI agents who would have been crucial witnesses falsely claimed they were not present and nothing further happened. On April 5, 1968, police raided the Los Angeles, California SNCC office while staffers were attending a memorial service for Martin Luther King.

Surveillance of movement activists, not only of SNCC, and harassment, including even by the Internal Revenue Service on alleged tax violations, became ever more intense. The government's strategy immobilized resources as activists were forced to divert attention to legal issues. COINTELPRO and other government actions (including the use of *agents provocateurs*) contributed greatly to creating an atmosphere of distrust within SNCC and between it and other organizations.

For many people almost regardless of political affiliation the country seemed to be falling apart in the Spring and Summer of 1968. The assassination of Martin Luther King Jr. on April 4 was followed by the shooting of Robert F. Kennedy, the younger brother of the assassinated President John F. Kennedy, on June 5. On July 23, in Cleveland, Ohio, "For the first time in the series of racial clashes that began in 1964, a group of heavily armed black men engaged in a shoot-out with the police. It was not a riot. It was armed, guerrilla warfare."[13] Shooting and arson went on for five days. Seven people were killed, including three police officers.

Protests against the Vietnam War continued unabated in 1968, mainly at universities, and here too police repression became more common. In April, SDS and the Student Afro-American Society seized several Columbia University (New York City) buildings to protest University involvement with war contracts, and its attempts to seize a section of a nearby largely Black neighborhood in order to build a gymnasium. On April 3, after days of fruitless negotiations, the city police proceeded to evict the students. The Black students surrendered and were arrested. The white students, in other buildings, resisted. There was considerable police brutality, about seven hundred arrests, and more than a hundred injured including some police. In May there was more police violence after another sit-in.

There were more than 3,000 campus protests that Spring; a number were conducted by Black students around issues affecting mainly the Black community, but most were protests against the war. It was the high point of Students for a Democratic Society's history. (Yet, just a year later, beset by internal factionalism, SDS splintered and for all practical purposes collapsed.)

Later, in August at the 1968 Democratic Party Presidential Convention, a number of anti-war groups including SDS marched to the convention hotel only to be confronted by thousands of city police, the National Guard, and units of the regular army. The scenes of tear gas and clubbing's, and the reactions inside the convention as the tear gas seeped in, were widely seen on television. "The nature of the response was unrestrained and indiscriminate police violence made all the more shocking by the fact that it was often inflicted upon persons who had broken no law, made no threat. These included peaceful demonstrators, onlookers, and large numbers of residents who were simply passing through"[14]A CORE activist summarized the widespread sense on the part of many of her brothers and sisters in "the movement": "The committed found themselves utterly alone. When one considers the large number of liberals and semi-radicals, Black and white, who had continued, in the face of all evidence to the contrary, to believe fervently in reform and education as the only practical road toward the solution to the domestic crises we face, we can see clearly the significance of 1968 in eliminating this approach as a realistic possibility. In short, they had become revolutionaries."[15]

Public opinion polls revealed, however, that the general public supported the police actions in Chicago.

There was widespread hostility, especially within the white working class, towards students, minorities, and welfare recipients. The Republican candidate, Richard Nixon, manipulated this sentiment and ran on a "law and order" platform. He won the election that November. Eight Chicago protesters were later tried for conspiracy to commit a riot. They included a well-known pacifist, a leading member of SDS, and Bobby Seale, the co-founder of the Black Panther Party. The trial went on for five months; convictions were ultimately overturned or, in a few cases, sentences were suspended for time served.

The scent of teargas and the threat and actuality of violence, it appeared, was everywhere. By the end of July 1968, there had been at minimum eight bombings and burnings of Selective Service (conscription offices) or military facilities in the U.S. presumably to impede the war effort. It was widely assumed, within the peace movement, that some of this was carried out by police agents or civilians in their employ.

Urban guerrilla warfare now became a topic of conversation both within radical Black circles and among white sympathizers, as well as within police and military circles. The left-wing journalist I.F. Stone, in his weekly newsletter, commented on August 19, 1968, that "we face a black revolt; that the black ghettos regard the white police as an occupying army that guerrilla warfare against this army has begun" In the January 1968 *Army* magazine, a Colonel Robert B. Rigg predicted that "in the next decade at least one major metropolitan area could be faced with guerrilla warfare requiring sizable United States army elements." Local police forces developed elaborate contingency plans, special tactical units, and the latest in counter-insurgency weaponry to deal with the feared onslaught of Black guerrillas. On the ultra-right, the John Birch Society, the Minutemen, the Klan, and similar groups were also preparing for race war.[16]

This was the context in which SNCC staff met that December in Atlanta. Between repression, defections, expulsions, and more fundamentally its failure to maintain its mass base in the South, SNCC's very survival was now in question. It turned out to be the beginning of the end.

Chapter 5
Closing the File

"We are dedicated to building a socialist society inside the United States where the total means of production and distribution are in the hands of the state and that must be led by revolutionary blacks. Only by armed, well-disciplined black-controlled government can we ensure the stamping out of racism in this country.[1]
James Forman, April, 1969.

"Rap" Brown was now effectively immobilized by his legal problems. The short-term solution was to create a collective leadership of nine deputy chairmen (few women were still in the organization). The Program Secretary, Phil Hutchings became de facto the official spokesperson after SNCC's June 1968 staff meeting. Hutchings' views came from his background as a northern, urban organizer, and he argued that Blacks needed to go beyond rioting and create a Black political party that would confront both racial and class issues. "If you are talking about really going for power, and not simply some kind of cultural faddism, you have to talk about overturning the capitalist power system," he said.[2] However, SNCC was hardly in a position to promote such an ambitious agenda since its membership was shrinking by the day. It was shortly after this meeting that Carmichael was expelled.

According to FBI files, there were 28 in attendance at the next staff meeting in Atlanta in December 1968 (including two agents), but only six were old-timers. Two of them, Willie Ricks, the originator of the Black Power slogan, and Cleveland Sellers, who was facing prison for refusing military service, had maintained contact with Carmichael and the Panthers, and when they refused to organize an armed alternative unit to the Panthers they were expelled and later physically threatened. Although Forman was present, he could do nothing since he had just returned from a much-needed rest in the Caribbean, and the remaining staff doubted his leadership capacity.

Forman understood that SNCC faced perhaps its final crisis. He saw that the 1965 Voting Rights Act had forced SNCC into a historical impasse: If it failed to develop a new strategy, it would continue its decline. In a 1967 paper entitled "Rock Bottom," he had argued that reforms such as voting rights and segregation in public accommodations were no longer the issue. Rather, he said, "rock bottom" problems ranging from unemployment to "the malignant nature of America's racist foreign policy" should be addressed.[3] Given SNCC's weaknesses, he had already begun to explore alternative strategies. In early 1968 he was invited to Detroit to look into the work of a new organization, the League of Revolutionary Black Workers. He was also invited to speak at a National Black Economic Development Conference that was to take place in Detroit the following April.

The League was the outgrowth of efforts by Black workers in Detroit automobile plants to protest a variety of grievances including discrimination in job assignments and promotions. In May 1968, there was a "wildcat" (not authorized by the United Automobile Workers union) strike at a Dodge plant. This led to the creation of the Dodge Revolutionary Union Movement (DRUM). In January 1969, a wildcat strike at Chrysler's

Eldon Avenue plant led to ELRUM, followed by several other "RUMs", not all of them in auto. These groups consolidated as the League. The leadership was Marxist-oriented, influenced by generations of leftist activists both Black and white in Detroit, a city that some on the left considered the "Petrograd" of the United States. Forman saw the League as the logical successor to SNCC.

The National Black Economic Development Conference, sponsored initially by Protestant church organizations to encourage Black businesses, was taken over by the League. It dominated the steering (executive) committee. Together with Forman, the committee wrote a "Black Manifesto" calling for reparations in the form of funding to Black organizations to be paid by white churches and synagogues. Although the Manifesto was extreme in tone, with talk of revolution and "long years of sustained guerrilla warfare," the actual demand for a half billion dollars was little different from similar "demands" by other black organizations. Its tone, however, drew the attention of the FBI.[4]

On May 4, 1969, Forman disrupted a religious service at the progressive Riverside Church in New York City to present his reparations demand. The audience was dumbfounded. Some walked out, others wept. Forman complained that while Germany was paying reparations to Jews, Blacks had been paid nothing for their deaths during slavery. A number of financial grants were subsequently made to various organizations including DRUM and the League, but far short of $500 million. When Forman went to SNCC at its staff meeting in June 1969 for support for the reparations project he was rebuffed.

It was at this meeting that Rap Brown reasserted his leadership following a chaotic period with a collective executive. He proposed that SNCC change its name to Black Revolutionary Action Party and become a quasi-military group like the Panthers. Forman opposed this strategy probably because it ran counter to the strategy of organizing Black workers. Lacking any support, he resigned. A month later, Brown called a press conference and announced that SNCC had now been reconstituted as the Student National Coordinating Committee, permanently dropping the nonviolent label, which in substance had long since been abandoned.

Forman, who was writing a book on Franz Fanon, increasingly saw the Black struggle in the U.S.A. as part of a third-world revolutionary movement towards socialism in which "the workers, the poor farmers, and all the other wretched of the American earth have control, and in which the vanguard of revolutionary change will be Black people, Indians, Chicanos, Puerto Ricans, Orientals."[5] He stayed with the League of Revolutionary Black Workers for some time. Despite its initial successes the League soon ran aground. In addition to internal disputes, in particular between members who oriented to "Marxism-Leninism" and alliances with white radical organizations versus those advocating an independent Black strategy, the League faced the hostility of most white workers, the United Auto Workers union officialdom (including its Black officials), and law enforcement agencies. Efforts to expand nationally in the form of a Black Workers Congress failed. The League struggled on into the 1970s, suffered a series of splits, and finally expired, even though many of its members went on to be active in social change organizations and in electoral politics. Fundamentally, even had the League survived, the collapse of the Detroit automobile industry would have called into question any chance of long-term success at least among industrial workers in Detroit and other "rust belt" deindustrialization cities of the Middle West.

Rap Brown still faced trial on gun charges in Maryland going into 1970. On March 9, the day before his scheduled trial, William "Che" Payne and Ralph Featherstone, who were to pick Brown up and take him to the court, were both killed when a bomb in their car exploded. Brown then disappeared, going underground in Canada, but then in an episode still unexplained was wounded in a gun battle with New York police following a robbery. He served five years in the notorious Attica prison, where he converted to Islam, changing his name to Jamil Abdullah Al-Amin. After his release, he moved to Georgia where, in 2002, he was convicted of murdering a Black police officer and sentenced to life imprisonment.

After the killing of the two SNCC workers, organizing activity virtually ceased. Purges and resignations among the remaining members continued. The FBI reported, in May 1971, that in recent months SNCC had not "participated in any demonstration or disruptive activity, and it is believed incapable of accomplishing same in view of the limited membership, lack of funds and internal dissension."[6]

There was a brief flurry of SNCC activity in the form of the Black Women's Liberation Committee, founded actually in 1968 by, among others, Frances Beal, a SNCC staffer. That group soon became autonomous. The BWLC evolved into the Third World Women's Alliance, which lasted from 1970 to 1978.

Fanon Che Wilkins (whose parents had been SNCC activists) wrote that former SNCC activists also played a role in organizing the Sixth Pan-African Congress, which was held in Dar es Salaam in June 1974. Courtland Cox, who had been a central figure in SNCC, served in the Secretariat of the planning group for the Congress.[7] Cox had also been involved with a Washington, D.C. bookstore called Drum and Spear, which was devoted to Black and African literature and ran educational sessions. It was founded by a former SNCC worker, Charlie Cobb, in 1968. It went out of business in 1974.

White SNCC and, later, ex-SNCC workers also launched several attempts, with varying degrees of success, to organize among the white poor in the South. This began in the spring of 1964 with the founding of the mostly white Southern Student Organizing Committee. Several of its members, including some from Students for a Democratic Society (SDS), worked in white communities in Mississippi. Their emblem consisted of a black and a white handshake superimposed on the Stars and Bars Confederate flag. Emmie Schrader Adams, a white SNCC worker, went alone to rural northeast Mississippi in an attempt to organize poor white farmers. This effort failed when she was exposed as a COFO worker, which put a (figurative and perhaps literal) target on her back. She recalls that in 1966, as the role of whites in SNCC came into question, they were told to work in the white community, but this "was often a smokescreen for 'Get Lost!' Why kid ourselves about this?"[8]

More successful was a campaign organized by Bob Zellner and his wife Dottie, called GROW (Grass Roots Organizing Work), which organized some woodcutters, factory workers, and poultry processing workers, both Black and white. Zellner had proposed that this be an official SNCC project, but since his days with SNCC were really over, the project proceeded without SNCC sponsorship. The Zellners located the project in New Orleans. They recruited several white former SNCC and SDS members and plunged into an attempt, almost unthinkable at that time, to promote interracial labor actions. They had to deal with some union members who were at the same time active in the KKK. The project lasted about ten years, leaving behind a number of trained union activists.

These were among the many, many residual effects as former SNCC workers scattered throughout the world, from San Francisco to, literally, Budapest, and probably even farther, to carry on SNCC's original mission to fight for human rights in one form or another.

But SNCC as an organization was over.

Chapter 6
Conclusion: The Band of Brothers and Sisters

*The new FBI Building on Echelon Parkway in Jackson,
Mississippi was dedicated on June 21, 2011. It was
named after James Chaney, Andrew Goodman and
Michael Schwerner, the first martyrs of Freedom
Summer. Added to these names was that of Roy K.
Moore, the Field Director of the FBI in Jackson, in
charge of the investigation in 1964. The naming was the
result of legislation sponsored by Bennie G. Thompson,
the Black Congressman from Mississippi's Second
District, who had been an SNCC worker. The Bill was
signed by President Obama.*

SNCC is the story of how a small series of local
civil rights protests developed into a large nonviolent
direct-action movement, and how those who led it turned
it into a revolutionary Black Power cadre organization.
SNCC was destroyed by a combination of strategic errors
and miscalculations, internal discord, external
repression, and indirectly by its own successes.

SNCC's activities in voter registration campaigns and
in the formation of the Mississippi Freedom Democratic
Party led to increasingly effective Black political
participation and the gaining of political offices in parts
of the South where there had been no Black officials
since the Reconstruction Period (1867-1877). These
campaigns challenged the racist exclusion of Blacks from
the Southern Democratic Party. Later came such issues
as increasing the minimum wage and even abolishing the
death penalty, which were far in advance of the National
Democratic Party. SNCC helped to organize the

Mississippi Freedom Labor Union with several thousand members, mainly among day laborers in cotton fields. The MFLU advocated a number of reforms including equality in wages and job opportunities. SNCC was also involved in the campaign for "home rule" in Washington, D.C., which was then directly under the rule of the U.S. Congress and had no independent political power. (It has some limited powers today but is still not represented by a voting Congressperson). SNCC supported and worked for numerous Black candidates for public office, including the U.S. Congress, in Georgia, Alabama, Virginia, and North Carolina. The Voting Rights Act of 1965, promoted by President Johnson, would not have been possible without SNCC, although of course other civil rights organizations were also involved.

However, as Cleveland Sellers of SNCC put it, "When the federal government passed bills that supposedly supported Black voting and outlawed segregation, SNCC lost the initiative in those areas."[1] A number of SNCC workers had trouble adjusting to roles in various anti-poverty programs. "They sneered at professional reformers who worked regular hours and submitted to organizational restraints."[2] In November 1965, some of the more pragmatically-oriented SNCC workers left to work with the MFDP, which others saw as in danger of taking on the very values of the political system it was designed to change. But SNCC's own organizing efforts were lagging by then and failing to produce clear benefits to Blacks both in its Northern campaigns and in the South. Supporters, including financial, were drifting away. Strategic differences between SNCC and the Southern Christian Leadership Conference grew during and after the Selma march. One activist with the Congress of Racial Equality (CORE) wrote, "By the close of 1965, the compounded conflicts had reached the point of no return: communication between various elements of the movement had become virtually nonexistent, diminishing contributions and widening schisms between North and South, Black and white, poor and not poor; (these) took their final toll."[3]

SNCC faced some strategic decisions at the height of its strength, following the voter registration campaign in Mississippi ("Freedom Summer"), in 1964. It had at that time a large body of organizers, many followers, and a reputation for courage and determination. SNCC might have chosen to continue to work through political avenues such as electoral politics and disciplined nonviolent demonstrations. No-one forced SNCC to move in the kind of radical direction that would inevitably lead to clashes with the political state that it was bound to lose. No-one forced SNCC to replace the "freedom now" slogan with "Black Power" in June 1966, during the march supporting James Meredith after he had been shot.[4] It was at this point that John Lewis and other advocates of nonviolence began to distance themselves from SNCC, and when liberal and mainstream civil rights organizational financial support began to dry up.

But could SNCC really have gone a more conventional route, thus avoiding repression and perhaps again becoming a major factor in civil rights and American politics more generally? Many of its staff and its followers, after abandoning SNCC did, after all, continue the fight for equal rights through participation in the Democratic Party and in mainstream civil rights organizations. Julian Bond, one of SNCC's founders, was later elected to three terms as President of the NAACP. On the other hand, SNCC's experience of conventional politics, of step-by-step reform, of attempts to work within the Democratic Party (as when it tried to have the MFDP seated at the 1964 Atlantic City Democratic Party convention), led many SNCC workers to conclude that traditional ways (including the nonviolent and religious-based strategy of King and the SCLC) led nowhere, or at best to gains so minimal that they could be considered little more than trickery. The conditions of everyday life, especially for the many Black poor, were still too desperate to accept crumbs. Voting did little to change the economic picture. Nor can it be argued, given the evidence, that the government would have left SNCC alone even if it had gone a more "respectable" route; all the mainstream civil rights organizations were not only under surveillance but, as in Martin Luther King's case, the victims of government-planted rumors intended to disrupt completely legal activities. The FBI under J. Edgar Hoover made little distinction between the respectable and the revolutionary among Black activists.

After 1964 SNCC, rather than following any sort of thought-out political strategy to cope with new conditions, seemed to lurch forward step by step, each step of its apparent choosing closing off alliances and financial support and leading to further isolation. If it had a strategy, it was to mistake state repression for a sign of weakness on the part of the power structure. It failed to see that repression together with its partner, cooptation, indicated strength even as the American war in Vietnam intensified and peace forces against the war grew more militant. In this SNCC was not alone. The Black Panther Party, as well as segments of Students for a Democratic Society (SDS) and some other New Left groups, also made this mistake. For a few older observers on the Left, this did not come as a surprise. It would have been difficult for most of the relatively theoretically naive members of SNCC (some of whom rejected most theory, especially Marxism, as "white") to have clearly understood that state repression was at that moment a sign of strength and not weakness, that the revolution was not around the corner. But SNCC only slowly came to understand that repression as carried out by the political structure via local police and the national FBI was undergirded by a "well-organized white conservative backlash against Black activism" in particular against advocates of Black Power.[5] SNCC workers "refused to soften the tone of their rhetoric even while recognizing that outspoken militancy often unified whites in support of police repression while dividing Blacks."[6]

Bob Zellner summarized the dilemma: SNCC began by working with three important and effective tools. One was nonviolent direct action, religiously motivated, superbly suited for public relations (outside the South and throughout the entire observant world) and effective in changing "race relations" in Upper Southern states in significant ways, if not completely. The second, also important in public relations and fundraising, was its interracial composition. The third was its commitment to long-term community organizing and the training of local leaders. The first was displaced with an acceptance, initially only informally but finally with full commitment of armed defense. The second was finally abandoned in December 1966, when whites were excluded from

SNCC's leadership. The third, grass-roots organizing, was gradually whittled away by the "defection" of SNCC workers to more established anti-poverty programs, Democratic Party-political activity, and almost needless to say, battle fatigue. As more and more SNCC workers abandoned the organization to take the route of working in reform campaigns, the remaining militants felt increasingly isolated, yet were left more convinced than ever that the revolutionary road was correct. In that they were joined by a fraction of the anti-war Students for a Democratic Society (culminating in the Weather Underground) and the Black Panther Party (which did at least organize some free breakfast programs). However, that revolutionary rhetoric led even further to the abandonment of SNCC by liberal and mainstream civil rights organizations.

Contributing to this abandonment, Zellner argued, were two radical decisions that many, perhaps most, liberals could not countenance at that time: SNCC was the first civil rights organization actively to oppose the war, even to the point of advocating draft resistance. Martin Luther King Jr. came out against the war later and also suffered the loss of support of many liberal and labor allies as a result. And, many Jewish supporters turned away because of SNCC's publishing an article supporting Palestinians' right to self-determination even though this was not an official position. Three decisions, the expulsion of whites, Vietnam, and Palestine, Zellner argued, "together spelled the eventual doom of the organization." [7]

Yet SNCC's sympathies with the Palestinian people should not have come as a surprise since by 1967 SNCC had become, in its own view, part of the worldwide anti-imperialist cause. As James Forman, perhaps SNCC's most thoughtful leader, saw it later, "For SNCC to see the struggle against racism, capitalism, and imperialism as being indivisible made it inevitable for SNCC to take a position against the greatest imperialist power in the Middle East, and in favor of liberation and dignity for the Arab people."[8] Compromise on this issue would have been considered a betrayal of the anti-imperialist cause.

The effects of repression, in the view not only of movement participants but also of almost all observers, cannot be underestimated when considering SNCC's gradual demise. A reign of terror with regard to all civil rights activists prevailed in much of the Lower South. The civil rights movement overall suffered at least 200 murders from 1951 to 1968. SNCC offices were under constant surveillance. Following demonstrations in the South SNCC workers were frequently arrested and charged with inciting a riot. Police raided SNCC offices even in the North, leading to the gradual collapse of community organizing. As Lewis Killian, a white sociologist of Southern background long involved with civil rights activities observed, insurgency "has subsided not because the racial crisis has passed but because white power has demonstrated that open black defiance is extremely dangerous and often suicidal. The ranks of the most dramatically defiant Black leaders were decimated by imprisonment, emigration, and assassination"[9] Surely this contributed to the exhaustion of older members (and the lack of a cohort of younger militants to replace them, since the average member participated no more than one year). Membership declined dramatically after 1966.[10]

The Black Panther Party was the extreme example of this repression. The Chicago Police killed Panthers Fred Hampton and Panther Mark Clark during a raid on Dec. 4, 1969. From March 1968 to December 1969, 19 Panthers and sympathizers were killed. There were shootouts and endless arrests and trials. Yet in 1970 the BPP still had offices in 68 cities. The Party's strategy of armed defense was a direct challenge to police forces. SNCC and the BPP both suffered from repression and infighting, but the Party's schisms were more severe, to say the least. By 1971 the BPP leadership was split between those advocating community-based reforms such as breakfast programs, and the armed self-defense "insurrectionists" who accused the former of opportunism. Here too cooptation played a role. Government-sponsored breakfast programs had grown as part of President Johnson's "War on Poverty," undercutting the Panthers' reformist wing. The BPP, according to numerous published memoirs, then veered into criminality by the late 1970s and closed down altogether in 1982.[11] Huey P. Newton, one of the BPP founders and its chief for several years was shot to death in Oakland on Aug. 22, 1989, apparently the victim of a drug deal gone bad.

How much did the slogan of Black Power and more generally the rhetoric of Black Nationalism and separatism (not only by SNCC) contribute to the defection of liberal organizations and to the "white backlash" that led to the victory of the Republican Party in 1968 and subsequent years? Countryman argues that Black Power as it was carried out in practice (and in Carmichael's original meaning) succeeded in constructing "a vital and effective social movement that

71

remade the political and cultural landscape of American cities during the late 1960s and 1970s in ways that postwar liberalism could not and did not accomplish," by mobilizing the Black vote and electing Black politicians. Yet this strategy failed to accomplish major changes in the living and working conditions of many if not most Black families because of "urban deindustrialization and of suburban anti-tax politics."[12] But that anti-tax sentiment was itself a component of white backlash against the "welfare state," or welfare programs designed to assist the poor, which many whites saw as benefiting the "undeserving" welfare-receiving (and mostly Black, in the white public's incorrect perception) poor. In fact, if we consider the internal colony model, the skin color of mayors and other public officials did not matter. They were constrained in their ability to create change, just as their liberal reform white predecessors had been. In this context, neither the conventional civil rights organizations nor the more militant groups such as SNCC and CORE could be effective, and Black urban politics seemed to have little relevance to significant social change.

With the election of Barack Obama, it was hoped by many that he would take action to ameliorate the continuing economic stagnation in many Black communities and challenge the "prison-industrial complex" and the way police target young Black men. But he proved to be a disappointment. Obama failed to protest the acquittal of the man who killed Trayvon Martin in Florida in 2013, as he had failed to intervene in the execution of Troy Davis in Georgia in 2011. Soon #BlackLivesMatter came along to help fill a void in Black political organizing left by the demise of SNCC and other militant groups some forty years earlier. BLM grew rapidly following the shooting of Michael Brown in Ferguson, Missouri on August 8, 2014. Its component local groups avoided entanglement with the mainstream civil rights organizations seen by the Black youth in BLM as "too little, too late."

BLM demands ranged from basic reforms that had been around for a long time, such as body cameras and better police training to the demand among some Black groups and white Left organizations to "abolish the police." This was controversial even within Black communities. It was seized on by white conservatives and of course, police unions in order to smear all efforts at changing policing in any way.

The movement's multiple component organizations and its decentralized and proudly leaderless structure (similar to Occupy Wall Street and its offshoots), using the tools of social media and large-scale demonstrations brought attention to every new police atrocity, so much so that even the mainstream media have been forced to pay attention. Today literally every police killing of a Black person makes headlines and triggers investigations. Police shootings of whites do not, even though in absolute numbers there are more of them.

This movement has not yet translated into the kind of social changes that came from the civil rights movement of the 1960s, much less moved beyond reforms to a deeper challenge to the social system.

*

Did SNCC fail? By the mid-1970s, with Black Nationalism still on the rise, many Black university students dismissed the nonviolent integrationist movement, including SNCC (by then gone from the scene) and Martin Luther King Jr. (also gone) as having been irrelevant to the long-term goal of full equality, not to mention liberation as a people or nation. This view is surely simplistic. On a day-to-day level by the mid-1970s the South was a vastly different place compared to just ten, and certainly twenty years before. "In the South," as Piven and Cloward said in 1977, "the deepest meaning of the winning of democratic rights is that the historical primacy of terror as a means of social control has been substantially diminished. The reduction of terror in the everyday life of a people is always in itself an important gain."[13] The diminishment of terror went hand in hand with the undermining of segregation in many dimensions of public life. "The South," noted Aldon Morris, a Black sociologist, "is a different place today Southern Blacks now live in a world that does not automatically strip them of human dignity."[14] SNCC was central to this progressive development.

The civil rights movement overall was never intended to be more than a reform struggle, except in the eyes of the radicals in SNCC, CORE, the Black Panther Party, the League of Revolutionary Black Workers, and Malcolm X. Martin Luther King Jr. and the handful of his adherents who saw the philosophy of nonviolence as a way of life more than merely a tactic, intended the movement to go far beyond integration as a goal. All of these understood in some way that if real equality in all spheres of life, including the economic dimension, was to be achieved for the mass of the Black population,

74

nothing short of a revolutionary change in the social system would be required. The political state correctly understood and feared these elements of the civil rights struggle, and destroyed them piece by piece.

The reforms envisioned by civil rights activists decades before the 1960s have been substantially won. The revolutionary changes required for full equality and liberation from racism and oppression have not.

Appendix A
Timeline of Important SNCC and Related Events

Spring, 1941: March on Washington Movement (A. Philip Randolph)

May 17, 1954: Brown vs. Board of Education

Dec. 1, 1955-Nov. 13, 1956: Montgomery Bus Boycott (Martin Luther King, Jr.)

Mar. 7, 1956: Founding of the (White) Citizens Councils of America

Sept. 9, 1957: Civil Rights Act establishing Commission on Civil Rights passed (Eisenhower)

Aug. 1958: Sit-Ins in Oklahoma City, Okla. and Wichita, Kans.

Feb. 1, 1960: Sit-Ins in Greensboro, N.C. begin 1960s movement.

Mar. 1, 1960: Massive arrests in Orangeburg, S.C.

April 15-17, 1960: Founding conference establishing SNCC.

Oct. 19, 1960: Sit-in demonstrators including King arrested in Atlanta, Ga.

Nov. 8, 1960: Election of John F. Kennedy as President.

Jan. 1961: Black farmers in Fayette and Haywood Counties, Tenn. forced from farms.

May 4, 1961: Freedom Riders begin their ride from Washington, D.C.

May 14, 1961: Freedom Rider buses attacked in Anniston, Ala.

Fall, 1961: Albany, Ga. movement to desegregate bus and train facilities.

Sept. 30, 1962: James Meredith integrates University of Mississippi after white insurrection.

June 12, 1963: Medgar Evers of NAACP assassinated in Mississippi.

Aug. 28, 1963: March on Washington (King and civil rights organizations incl. SNCC)

Sept. 15, 1963: Birmingham, Ala. church bombing, 4 girls killed.

Nov. 22, 1963: President Kennedy assassinated.

June, 1964: Oxford, Ohio training for Freedom Summer voter registration project.

June 21, 1964: Three volunteers disappear after investigation black church burning. Bodies found Aug. 4.

July 2, 1964: Civil Rights Act of 1964 passed, promoting equal employment, etc. (Johnson)

July 18, 1964: Harlem, New York City riot begins new phase in "race relations."

Aug. 28, 1964: North Philadelphia, Pa. riot.

Aug. 24-28, 1964: Mississippi Freedom Democratic Party sends delegation to Democratic Party
Presidential Convention in Atlantic City, N.J.

Nov. 1964: SNCC staff meeting in Waveland, Miss. MFDP supports L.B. Johnson, who is elected.

Feb. 21, 1965: Malcolm X assassinated.

Mar. 7, 1965: Selma, Ala. March.

July 24, 1965: Detroit, Mich. Riots.

Aug. 6, 1965: Civil Rights Bill (voting rights) passed under Johnson.

Aug. 11-17, 1965: Watts, Los Angeles riots.

Aug. 1965: Founding of the Lowndes County (Ala.) Freedom Organization (later Black Panther Party).

Nov. 1965: Julian Bond wins seat in Georgia Assembly; is refused. U.S. Supreme Court. orders him installed.

Jan. 1966: Murder of Sammy Younge (SNCC); Assassination of Vernon Dahmer (NAACP).

May. 1966: Stokely Carmichael replaces John Lewis as SNCC chair.

June 5, 1966: James Meredith shot; Meredith march for voter registration continues. Black Power slogan introduced by SNCC.

Aug. 13, 1966: Police raid SNCC office in Philadelphia, Pa.

Dec. 1966: SNCC staff vote to exclude whites.

May 2, 1967: Armed Black Panthers stage go-in at California State Capital in Sacramento.

May. 1967: H. Rap Brown succeeds Stokely Carmichael as SNCC chair.

July 12-17, 1967: Newark, N.J. riots.

April 3, 1968: Columbia University sit-in broken by police attack.

April 4, 1968: Martin Luther King assassinated.

May. 1968: Formation of League of Revolutionary Black Workers in Detroit, Mich.

June 5, 1968: Robert F. Kennedy assassinated.

Aug. 28, 1968: Police attack demonstrators at Democratic Convention in Chicago, Ill.

June 4, 1969: James Forman disrupts Riverside Church service seeking reparations.

July. 1969: SNCC changes name to Student National Coordinating Committee.

Dec. 4, 1969: Panthers Hampton and Clark killed by police in Chicago, Ill.

Mar. 9, 1970: SNCC members Che Payne and Ralph Featherstone killed by bomb in their car.

May. 1971: FBI reports SNCC incapable of mounting any demonstrations or disruptive activity.

Dec. 1973: New York FBI closes file, no SNCC activity for several years and "future prospects for such are exceedingly faint."

Appendix B
SNCC Statement of Purpose

By James Lawson Jr.

(April 15-17, 1960, Shaw University)

We affirm the philosophical or religious ideal of nonviolence as the foundation of our purpose, the presupposition of our faith, and the manner of our action. Nonviolence as it grows from Judaic-Christian traditions seeks a social order of justice permeated by love. Integration of human endeavor represents the crucial first step towards such a society.

Through nonviolence, courage displaces fear, love transforms hate. Acceptance dissipates prejudice, hope ends despair. Peace dominates war, faith reconciles doubt. Mutual regard cancels enmity. Justice for all overthrows injustice. The redemptive community supersedes systems of gross social immorality.

Love is the central motif of nonviolence. Love is the force by which God binds man to himself and man to man. Such love goes to the extreme; it remains loving and forgiving even in the midst of hostility. It matches the rapacity of evil to inflict suffering with an *even more* enduring capacity to absorb evil, all the while persisting in love.

By appealing to conscience and standing on the moral nature of human existence, nonviolence nurtures the atmosphere in which reconciliation and justice become actual possibilities.

Appendix C
What is Black Power?

Was the slogan "Black Power" just rhetoric? It provided a cathartic outlet for younger Blacks especially but not only in Northern communities, in part because it scared a lot of whites. Its adoption by SNCC contributed to changing its image from a Southern to a national organization. Its militant tone promoted a revived sense of organizing possibilities. At the same time established civil rights groups could, by disavowing it, boost their organizations as respectable negotiators for Black objectives. The NAACP condemned it as "anti-white." The problem was that absent any detailed description by Carmichael or others, it could mean anything from traditional Black self-improvement efforts, ranging from those sponsored by Black churches or the Black Muslims of Elijah Muhammad and the Nation of Islam to Black cultural nationalists striving to promote an interest in Africa and African languages instruction. It helped lead to the demands by Black students for Black studies programs in universities. It could as well be used by separatists calling for a Black state, or just to the simple notion that Blacks should support Black candidates for public office. It was entirely consistent with the promotion of Black entrepreneurship, a tradition going back to pre-civil war days. Implied, and sometimes stated explicitly, was that it meant Black Nationalism, the conception that Blacks constituted an oppressed nation within a nation.

In the Spring of 1966, following the election of Stokely Carmichael as SNCC president, the Atlanta Project of SNCC developed a position paper explaining

"The Basis of Black Power." It was not an official SNCC statement, but it was widely accepted as indicative of SNCC's turn from "civil rights" (integrationism) to Black power. The paper proposed that Blacks organize Blacks, whites organize whites, and that SNCC should henceforth be entirely Black-staffed, Black-controlled, and Black-financed. "If we continue to rely upon white financial support, we will find ourselves entwined in the tentacles of the white power complex that controls this country," the paper stated. The reality, in the view of SNCC's paper, is that "when we view the masses of white people, we view in reality 180 million racists." In December 1966, the last white SNCC staff were told to leave.

The paper was "culturalist" in its approach: it concentrated on the incapacity of whites truly to understand the Black condition, and that "any re-evaluation will, for the most part, deal with identification. Who are Black people, what are Black people, what is their relationship to America and the world?"

Very soon, however, Carmichael and others began to provide more explicit content to the slogan and add a deeper analysis. Fundamentally it meant, for him, self-determination for Blacks in the dimensions of culture (their identity), economics (their sources of income and wealth) and politics (their political control over their communities). In 1967 he wrote, with political scientist Charles V. Hamilton, *Black Power, the Politics of Liberation in America.*[1] In this book Carmichael and Hamilton adopt a Black Nationalist theory, that "black

---

[1] (Random House, Vintage Books)

people in this country form a colony they stand as colonial subjects in relation to white society. Thus institutional racism has another name: colonialism." [2] This fit in perfectly with SNCC's identification with third-world anti-imperialist struggles, briefly foreshadowed in the Black Power position paper.

Although they did not mean colony in a literal sense, the Black ghettos of the U.S. do share some of the characteristics of classical colonies, especially "a relationship by which members of the colonized group tend to be administered by representatives of the dominant power," as white sociologist Robert Blauner explained.[3]

This "internal colony" thesis has some plausibility. Black labor is "exported" to work in the homes, factories, stores, and offices of white society; their bourgeoisie is small and dependent on outside capital; the ghetto infrastructure of education, social welfare, policing, and housing is controlled from the outside; and there is no Black-owned major capitalist enterprise that could provide significant employment. Even the sweatshops are owned by outsiders; even the drug trade is controlled by outside gangsters for the most part. In those cities where Blacks once worked in manufacturing, the factories are gone, the work "outsourced" abroad, or in the case of office work, to the suburbs. Yet the prescriptions by advocates were limited

---

[2] P. 5.
[3] Robert Blauner, "Internal Colonialism and Ghetto Revolt," *Social Problems* v. 16 no. 4 (Spring, 1969), p.396.

to building a Black political power base, community control of schools, control of poverty programs, and possibly even the creation of indigenous police forces. There was no fundamental critique of the capitalist roots of ghetto misery.

Within a few short years, however, at least some of SNCC's leading figures went far beyond this limited analysis, becoming much more explicitly revolutionary and socialist. By then, however, SNCC was on its last legs.

Today, when a dozen cities have Black-dominated political structures, and when Blacks are fully represented in most urban police forces, when a dozen Black congressional districts send Black representatives to Washington, the weakness of the theory is evident. Capital investment is still lacking. White-dominated industries that employed Black workers have "deindustrialized" many urban areas, leaving the Black community without sources of stable employment and with inadequate tax sources. Black mayors and their police forces play the role of social control agents as unemployment and the growth of the "informal economy" of drugs increases and the infrastructure of social support institutions is overwhelmed. Those Blacks who are financially able, abandon the ghettos to find better surroundings, especially schools, in the suburbs. As in "third world" countries, the poverty we see is not the result of a lack of development. It is, rather, the consequence of a particular kind of development (the development of underdevelopment we might say) stemming from the workings of American capitalism in the era of globalization.

Appendix D
List of Sources

Abu-Jamal, Mumia. *We Want Freedom*. South End Press, 2004.

Bibliotek des Wider stands. *Rebels with a Cause.* Laika Verlag, Hamburg, 2010.

Blauner, Robert. "Internal Colonialism and Ghetto Revolt," *Social Problems* 16#4 (Spring 1969).

Bloom, Joshua, & Martin, Waldo E. Jr. *Black Against Empire.* U. Cal. Press, 213.

Bond, Julian. "SNCC: What We Did," *Monthly Review* 52#5 (Oct. 2000).

Branch, Taylor. *At Canaan's Edge.* Simon and Schuster, 2006.

Carmichael, Stokely, & Hamilton, Charles V. *Black Power.* Vintage Books, 1967.

Carson, Clayborne. *In Struggle: SNCC and the Black Awakening of the 1960s.* Harvard Univ.Press, 1981.

Churchill, Ward, & Vander Wall, Jim. *Agents of Repression: The FBI's Secret War Against the Black Panther Party and the American Indian Movement.* South End Press, 1988.

Countryman, Matthew J. *Up South: Civil Rights and Black Power in Philadelphia.* Univ. of Pennsylvania Press, 2006.

Cunningham, David. *Klansville, U.S.A.: The Rise and Fall of the Civil Rights Era Ku Klux Klan.* Oxford U. Press, 2013,

Doyle, William. *An American Insurrection.* Anchor Books, 2003.

Farber, Samuel. *Social Decay and Transformation,* Ch. 5. Lexington Books, 2000.

Forman, James. *The Making of Black Revolutionaries.* Univ. of Washington Press, 1977.

Georgakas, Dan. "League of Revolutionary Black Workers," in Buhle, Buhle, and Georgakas, *Encyclopedia of the American Left.* Oxford Univ. Press, 1988.

Geschwender, James A. *Class, Race, and Worker Insurgency: The League of Revolutionary Black Workers.* Cambridge Univ. Press, 1977.

Holsaert, Faith S. et al, *Hands on the Freedom Plow.* Univ. of Illinois Press, 2010.

Holt, Len. *The Summer That Didn't End: The Story of the Mississippi Civil Rights Project of 1964.* William Morrow, 1965, and Da Capo Press, 1992.

Jacobs, Paul, and Landau, Saul. *The New Radicals.* Vintage Books, 1966.

Louis, Debbie. *And We Are Not Saved.* Doubleday, 1970.

McAdam, Doug. *Political Process and the Development of Black Insurgency, 1930-1970.* Univ. of Chicago Press, 1982.

--------------------*Freedom Summer.* Oxford Univ. Press, 1990.

--------------------"The Decline of the Civil Rights Movement," in Jo Freeman and Victoria Johnson. *Waves of Protest: Social Movements Since the Sixties.* Rowman and Littlefield, 1999.

Masotti, Louis H. and Corsi, Jerome R. *Shoot-Out in Cleveland, A Report to the National Commission on the Causes and Prevention of Violence.* Bantam Books, 1969.

Morris, Aldon D. *The Origins of the Civil Rights Movement.* Free Press, 1985.

National Advisory Commission on Civil Disorders ("Kerner Commission") *Report.* Bantam Books, 1968.

Oppenheimer, Martin and Lakey, George. *A Manual for Direct Action.* Friends Peace Committee 1964 and Quadrangle Books, 1965.

Oppenheimer, *The Sit-In Movement of 1960.* Carlson Publishing, 1989.

----------------- *The Urban Guerrilla.* Quadrangle Books, 1969.

Piven, Frances Fox and Cloward, Richard. *Poor People's Movements.* Vintage, 1977.

Sellers, Cleveland. *The River of No Return: The Autobiography of a Black Militant and the Life and Death of SNCC.* Univ. of Mississippi Press, 1973, 1990.

Skolnick, Jerome H. *The Politics of Protest, A Report to the National Commission on the Causes and Prevention of Violence.* Bantam Books, 1969.

Stoper, Emily. "The Student Nonviolent Coordinating Committee: Rise and Fall of a Redemptive Organization," in Jo Freeman and Victoria Johnson (eds.) *Waves of Protest: Social Movements Since the Sixties."* Rowman and Littlefield, 1999.

Umoja, Akinyele O. "1964: The Beginning of the End of Nonviolence in the Mississippi Freedom Movement." *Radical History Review* No. 85 (Winter, 2003).

----------*We Will Shoot Back: Armed Resistance in the Mississippi Freedom Movement.* New York University Press, 2013.

Unger, Irwin. *The Movement: A History of the American New Left 1959-1972.* Dodd, Mead, 1974.

Wilkins, Fanon Che. "A Line of Steel," in Berger, Dan (ed.) *The Hidden 1970s.* Rutgers Univ.   Press, 2010.

Williams, Robert F. *Negroes With Guns.* Marzani & Munsell, 1962.

Young, Jean Smith. "Do Whatever You Are Big

Enough to Do." In Holsaert, Faith S. *et al* (eds.) *Hands On the Freedom Plow.* Univ. of Illinois Press, 2010.

Zellner, Bob. *The Wrong Side of Murder Creek.* New South Books, 2008.

Zinn, Howard. *SNCC, the New Abolitionists.* Beacon Press, 1964.

Footnotes

Chapter 1

1. Clayborne Carson, *In Struggle: SNCC and the Black Awakening of the 1960s* (Harvard U. Press, 1981), 298.

2. The Sit-Ins were a strategy in which groups of Blacks, mainly students, would occupy seats in restaurants and eating sections of department stores such as Woolworth's that did not serve Black people, and ask to be served. When ordered to leave they would not, until closing time. They would return the following days until, it was hoped, the policy would change. Similar strategies were used to challenge segregation in other facilities such as "white" churches, public swimming pools, libraries, and amusement parks.

3. Martin Oppenheimer, *The Sit-In Movement of 1960* (Carlson Publishing, 1989), 19.

4. Doug McAdam, *Freedom Summer* (Oxford U. Press, 1988,1990), 24-26.

5. They were: Ezell Blair, Jr., David Richmond, Franklin McCain, and Joseph McNeill.

Chapter 2

1. Martin Oppenheimer, *The Sit-In Movement of 1960.* (Carlson Publishing, 1989) p. 46.

2. Cleveland Sellers, *The River of No Return: the Autobiography of a Black Militant and the Life and Death of SNCC.* (Univ. Press of Mississippi, 1973, 1990) p. 38.

3. A tenant farmer rents the land owned by a landlord. A sharecropper uses the land of the landlord in exchange for a portion of the harvest. Either, in those days, could be evicted at the whim of the landlord with the support of the local sheriff.

4. Technically just "Citizens Councils," a federation of extremist racist organizations that grew up throughout the South to resist the U.S. Supreme Court school desegregation decisions; supposedly more "respectable" than the Ku Klux Klan.

5. A cadre organization consists of members who make a maximum commitment to the cause, often as full-time workers, as distinct from a general membership organization where the level of commitment by most members is minimal or temporary.

6. Carson, 1995, p.67.

7. James Forman, *The Making of Black Revolutionaries* (Univ. of Washington Press, 1997), p. 253.

8. Forman, p. 274.

9. Bob Zellner, *The Wrong Side of Murder Creek* (New South Books, 2008), Ch. 12.

10. Carson, p. 95.

11. Sellers, 1973, 1990, pp. 72-76.

12. For example: "Whenever the President considers that unlawful obstruction or rebellion against the authority of the United States make it impossible to enforce the laws of the United Statesby the ordinary course of judicial proceedings, he may call into Federal service and use such of the armed forces as he considers necessary to enforce those laws or to suppress the rebellion." In Len Holt, *The Summer That Didn't End: The Story of the Mississippi Civil Rights Project of 1964* (William Morrow, 1965 and Da Capo Press, 1992) p. 61. Also Holt, Appendix V.

13. Holt, p. 67 and Appendix I.

14. This can be found as Appendix D in McAdam (1990); also in Holt, Appendix II.

15. Holt, Ch. VII.

16. McAdam (1990), p. 121.

17. Sellers (1973, 1990), p. 111.

Chapter 3

1. Quoted in Sellers (1973, 1990), p. 166

2. Akinyele O. Umoja, "1964: The Beginning of the End of Nonviolence in the Mississippi Freedom Movement, *Radical History Review* (Winter, 2003), pp. 201-226.

3. Howard Zinn, *SNCC, the New Abolitionists* (Beacon Press, 1964).

4. Umoja, pp. 222-223.

5. Carson (1981), p. 145.

6. Carson, p. 144.

7. Faith S. Holsaert *et al*, *Hands On the Freedom Plow* (U. of Ill. Press, 2010), p. 249.

8. McAdam, p. 108.

9. Interview, Nov. 16, 2011.

10. McAdam, p. 107.

11. Sellers, p. 116.

12. Sellers, pp. 117-118.

13. Carson, pp. 158-161; Forman, pp. 441-161; Zinn, pp. 263-267.

14. Carson, p. 166.

15. Forman, p. 238.

16. Sellers, pp. 130-132.

17. William Doyle, *An American Insurrection* (Anchor, 2003).

18. Stokely Carmichael and Charles V. Hamilton, *Black Power: The Politics of Liberation in America* (Vintage Books, 1967), p. 5.4

Chapter 4

1. Matthew J. Countryman, *Up South, Civil Rights and Black Power in Philadelphia* (Univ. of Pennsylvania Press 2006) pp. 155 ff.

2. *Report of the National Advisory Committee on Civil Disorders* (1968), sometimes called the Kerner Commission after its chairperson, Otto Kerner, Governor of Illinois.

3. Paul Jacobs and Saul Landau, *The New Radicals* (Vintage, 1966), quoted in Doug McAdam, *Political Process and the Development of Black Insurgency, 1930-1970* (Univ. of Chicago Press, 1982) p. 191.

4. Countryman, pp. 211-218.

5. Forman, p. 470.

6. Countryman, p. 218.

7. Counterintelligence Program: "This program has as its objective the neutralization of black extremist groups, the prevention of violence by these groups and the prevention of coalition of black extremist organizations." FBI Memorandum. Reprinted in Ward Churchill and Jim Vander Wall, *Agents of Repression: The FBI's Secret War Against the Black Panther Party and the American Indian Movement* (South End Press, 1988), p. 38. Neutralization meant, according to FBI Director J. Edgar Hoover, efforts to "expose, disrupt, misdirect, discredit, or otherwise neutralize" groups including the Deacons for Defense and Justice, CORE, SNCC, and even the SCLC, plus

others such as the Nation of Islam. Tactics included collaborating with local police forces to arrest local leaders "on every possible charge," and to make efforts to discredit these groups in the eyes of the "responsible Negro Community." (Carson, pp. 262-263).

8. Carson, p.54.

9. Taylor Branch, *At Canaan's Edge* (Simon and Schuster, 2006), p. 606.

10. Forman, pp. 538-39.

11. Countryman, p. 288.

12. Sellers, p. 258. He began *The River of No Return* while serving seven months in jail after being shot, then arrested on multiple charges following the Orangeburg incident.

13. Louis H. Masotti and Jerome R. Corsi, *Shoot-Out in Cleveland, a Report Submitted to the National Commission on the Causes and Prevention of Violence,* May 1969, p. viii.

14. Jerome H. Skolnick, *The Politics of Protest, a Report to the National Commission on the Causes and Prevention of Violence* (Bantam Books, 1969), p. 246.

15. Debbie Louis, *And We Are Not Saved* (Doubleday, 1970), p. 345.

16. Martin Oppenheimer, *The Urban Guerrilla* (Quadrangle, 1969), ch. 7.

Chapter 5

1. Sellers, p. 262.

2. Carson, p. 291.

3. Forman, pp. 477-479; Carson, p. 235.

4. James A. Geschwender, *Class, Race, and Worker Insurgency: The League of Revolutionary Black Workers.* (Cambridge U. Press), pp. 143-146; Forman, pp. 545-549; Carson, pp. 294-295.

5. Carson, pp. 295-296; Forman, pp. 550-551.

6. Carson, p. 298.

7. Fanon Che Wilkins, "A Line of Steel," in Dan Berger (ed.), *The Hidden 1970s* (Rutgers Univ. Press, 2010) pp 98-99, 104.

8. Holsaert, *et al, Hands On the Freedom Plow*) pp. 420-424.

Chapter 6

1. Julian Bond, "SNCC: What We Did," *Monthly Review* (Oct. 2000, v. 52 no. 5).

2. Carson, pp. 172-173.

3. Debbie Louis, p. 219.

4. In 1962 Meredith was the first Black to attend the University of Mississippi. His successful effort to enroll required the use of 31,000 troops to put down an armed insurrection by whites. In June 1966 Meredith decided to walk from Memphis, Tennessee to Jackson, Mississippi to promote voter registration. On June 6 he was wounded by a sniper. SNCC, CORE and King decided to continue the march and utilize it to register Black voters along the route. The slogan "Black Power" was proposed by an SNCC field organizer, Willie Ricks, and was quickly supported by the SNCC leadership.

5. Countryman, p. 9.

6. Carson, p. 290.

7. Zellner, p. 294.

8. Forman, pp. 496-497.

9. Quoted by Doug McAdam, "The Decline of the Civil Rights Movement," in Jo Freeman and Victoria Johnson, *Waves of Protest: Social Movements Since the Sixties* (Rowman and Littlefield, 1999), p. 343.

10. In the SNCC website link "Veterans Roll Call," of a total of 483 activists from all civil rights groups who had enrolled themselves, more than one-third listed SNCC as at least one of their organizational affiliations. Of that group, less than five percent were active after 1966.

11. For an excellent analysis of this process, see Samuel Farber, *Social Decay and Transformation* (Lexington Books, 2000), Ch. 5.

12. Countryman, p. 9. Deindustrialization refers to the decline of manufacturing due in large part to the "export" of factories to the non-union South or abroad.

13. Frances Fox Piven and Richard A. Cloward, *Poor People's Movements* (Vintage, 1977), Ch. 4.

14. Aldon D. Morris, *The Origins of the Civil Rights Movement* (Free Press, 1985), p. 287.